A Contented House with Twins

A Contented House with Twins

Gina Ford and Alice Beer

Vermilion
LONDON

First published in the United Kingdom in 2006 by Vermilion, an imprint of
Ebury Publishing
Random House UK Ltd.
Random House
20 Vauxhall Bridge Road
London SW1V 2SA

Addresses for companies within the Random House Group can be found at
www.randomhouse.co.uk

Random House UK Limited Reg. No. 954009
www.randomhouse.co.uk

Penguin Random House is committed to a sustainable future for our business, our readers and our planet. This book is made from Forest Stewardship Council® certified paper.

ISBN 9780091906986

Printed and bound in Great Britain by Clays Ltd, St Ives plc

Please note that conversions to imperial weights and measures are suitable equivalents and not exact.

The information given in this book should not be treated as a substitute for qualified medical advice; always consult a medical practitioner. Neither the author nor the publisher can be held responsible for any loss or claim arising out of the use, or misuse, of the suggestions made or the failure to take medical advice.

Copies are available at special rates for bulk orders. Contact the sales development team on 020 7840 8487 or visit www.booksforpromotion.co.uk for more information.

To buy books by your favourite authors and register for offers, visit
www.randomhouse.co.uk

Contents

For Phoebe and Dora

Acknowledgements

We would like to thank our publisher, Fiona MacIntyre, for recognising the importance of this book and giving us the opportunity to write it; our editor, Imogen Fortes, and the rest of the Random House team for all their hard work and fantastic support.

Gina: My agent, Emma Kirby, deserves a big thank you for her help in getting our ideas onto paper and formatting the book. Also a very special thank you to Dawn Fozard for helping us pull the manuscript together, and to Yamini Franzini and all the members of contentedbaby.com who as mothers of twins gave us so many helpful suggestions of what they would like to see in the book.

Alice: Firstly I must thank Gina for guiding Paul and I through that exhausting but exhilarating first year. You are a feisty, wise and wonderful woman.

I would like to thank Mark Johnson at the Chelsea and Westminster Hospital for keeping Phoebe and Dora safe until they were ready to face the world.

Thank you to the Twin and Multiple Birth Association and the Multiple Births Foundation for their support and advice,

My thanks and love to my parents for constantly coming when we call and for their unconditional devotion to my little ones.

And my love and respect to Paul; a perfect Daddy who takes amazing care of his three girls and never ceases to give me butterflies. I adore you.

Introduction

My first book, *The Contented Little Baby Book*, was based on my experience of working with over 300 babies and their families. It very quickly became a bestseller through word of mouth recommendation and hundreds of thousands of parents around the world are now following my *CLB* routines. During my time as a maternity nurse, I also helped care for over 16 sets of twins, and advised hundreds more parents of twins. It was this experience, together with the feedback I get from parents through my consultancy work and my website, www.contentedbaby.com, that made me realise there was a real need to adapt the *CLB* routines for twins. And with the number of multiple births rising each year, it would seem there is now an even greater need.

I first met Alice when her babies were six months old, and was immediately impressed by the way she was following the *CLB* routines. It was obvious from the very beginning that she was a hands-on mum, who was managing to meet the needs of her babies in every way. Sharing our experiences of the highs and lows of caring for two babies quickly made us realise that combining my adaptation of the *CLB* routines with Alice's experience of using them would be of great benefit to parents of twins. The result is this book. Each chapter begins with Alice's account of the problems and successes she encountered with her own babies which is followed by my advice on raising contented little babies.

I have adapted my original routines on the basis that in the early days you will probably find it easier to feed or settle one twin before the other. The start times in the boxes at the beginning of each routine relate to the times you need to feed or settle the first twin and, as outlined in the routines themselves, you will need to do the same with the other twin 10 to 15 minutes later. Once you gain more confidence, however, you can adapt these times according to what suits your babies best.

Although at times having twins is undoubtedly more difficult than having just one baby, there is a huge amount of truth in the adage that twins are double the trouble but double the joy. I found it enormous fun working with twins and I hope that this book will enable help you to enjoy every minute with yours.

Gina Ford

~

If you are reading this book the chances are that you are expecting twins. Congratulations! It's a funny old journey you are starting, but I truly believe that we are the very lucky ones! Having twins is very special and through the exhaustion and complications somehow you will always remember that. Four years ago I was lying on my back with a 52-inch waist, yearning for a book like this, so I hope that with Gina's wisdom and Phoebe and Dora's inspiration we can help you on your way.

Expecting twins is, of course, never quite accurate. Yes, there were two little blobs on the scan but when the word 'twins' was mentioned, if I hadn't been horizontal you could have knocked me over with a pregnancy testing kit. This was not what we were expecting at all.

When my doctor first confirmed that I was pregnant, I had rushed to the bookshop and bought about five pregnancy manuals. When I discovered at seven weeks that it was twins, however, the books became largely irrelevant. The monthly photos of the smiling woman with one little lump looked nothing like my poor stretching body and the token 'twin chapter' at the back of some of the books told me little more than that they would probably come early and I would probably need to take it easy.

As I was only two capsules into the packet of folic acid tablets when the blue line appeared in the pregnancy testing kit, I had to kick-start my 'healthy baby routine'. I think this is even more important with two – many expectant mothers of twins will agree that you can literally feel the little minxes robbing you of every nutrient as the pregnancy progresses. More vital than the advice of the nutritionist was the order of my obstetrician to take it easy which, being a stubborn Taurean control freak, I obviously ignored.

In the fifth month of pregnancy my partner, Paul, and I flew to Australia for Christmas, came home, moved house and I shot off to Spain filming. My body was incredible – so strong, so vital, so fantastic in the way it was adapting to these little inhabitants. Unfortunately, my cervix was not so incredible. At 22 weeks, I was told that I would lose the babies if I did not take myself to bed and stay there for the next three months. I was in the middle of filming a series of *Hot Property* for Channel Five in Spain and immediately had to tell the series producer I couldn't get in a car to Heathrow, let alone fly to Malaga the next morning. Fortunately, when the chips were down and the lives of two little 'nearly babies' were at stake, even the most hardened television types didn't question what I had to do. They recalled all their researchers, camera crews and contestants back from Spain – and I went to bed.

Until now I had been concentrating on the pictures in the pregnancy books of the mother, obsessing about how much bigger than her I was. But now, under doctor's orders and with the lives of our babies at risk, I became obsessed by the pictures of embryos. They were 22 weeks when they started threatening to come out, and damn it I couldn't find a book or a doctor on the Internet that would tell me they could possibly survive an entrance into the world at that stage.

I was allowed out of bed for a scan once a week to maintain my health, and out of bed once a day to maintain my sanity. It seemed that every time I got vertical I got bigger and each week when I dressed for the hospital, it was touch and go what I was going to get into. At first I did suffer a little one-baby envy, sitting in the waiting room at the foetal medicine centre surrounded by mothers-to-be looking glamorous in their wrap-around dresses and little cropped cardigans. I had surgical stockings to stop me getting blood clots and Simon Cowell trousers from the second month. But soon, perhaps like many other mums of twins, I developed a perverse pride in my two-baby bump. I got great pleasure in announcing loudly at the reception desk: 'Alice Beer to see Professor Nicolaides WITH TWINS. Put that in your designer pipe and smoke it!'

As a geriatric mother-to-be (aged 37 at conception), and as someone who wants all information available on any given subject, we had several appointments and scans to establish the health and well-being of the babies. I realised that incubating two little people inside me was a very complex procedure. Twin pregnancies can be complicated. If, as was suggested to me, one of the babies had been very sick indeed, there was no chance of doing anything to help without risking the other baby. And to have an amniocentesis on one baby to see if there MIGHT be something wrong was out of the question if there was a chance of losing both babies as a result. Nobody can make those decisions or suffer those dilemmas for you – they are for the wakeful hours in the middle of the night. But the firm odds are that you will get what you desperately hope for: two perfect babies.

As I lay in bed, my beautiful babies obediently grew and grew, and so correspondingly did my phone bill. As a journalist who had fallen into television via investigative research, there wasn't a pebble left unturned in my quest for knowledge. I sought constant reassurance and advice from brilliant organisations: unnoticed by millions but a lifeline to a few. Look at the back of this book under Further reading for the details of people who are just quietly getting on with researching and reviewing exactly the information you need to know as the prospective parent of more than one.

Because I couldn't make it to the antenatal classes, I relied on regular visits from pregnant friends to sit on the end of my bed and update me. Although my family was fantastic and friends completely dependable, apart from chats with my little babes, the closest relationship I was forming in my duvet weeks was with food. I was constantly hungry and constantly eating. It was a struggle to get enough food on the bedside table to last me until Paul came home to make supper.

Tears were also a big feature in those bed-ridden months. Multiply all those pregnancy hormones by two and throw in some dodgy scan results and the threat of a very premature labour and you will have more salt than a back-to-back showing of *Bambi*.

Maybe because of my hormones, my increasing size or, perhaps, my body trying to relieve itself of the boredom of bed rest, I began to develop the most absurd side effects. About halfway through the sixth month my wrists started aching and my third and fourth fingers started tingling. 'Ahhh! Carpal tunnel syndrome,' declared my lovely obstetrician. Nice to have a name for my bizarre symptoms but it developed into a painful, debilitating condition that woke me at night and prevented me picking up my babies once they were born.

At about the beginning of the sixth month I was getting ready to go for my scan, when I noticed a peculiar-looking wart developing on the side of my face. 'Ahhhh! Lupus Vigan,' declared the doctor. Painless and gone by the girls' first Christmas, it ruined those glowing mother-just-given-birth photographs. Following routine early blood tests and another 'Ahhh!' I was declared to have a blood-clotting condition called Lydon Factor Five. I had survived 37 years without even knowing about it (I still can't spell it), but it resulted in a daily injection of heparin in my thigh.

In spite of all this, I reached the eighth month and my little girls were still hanging on in there. My obstetrician declared I could get out of bed. Frankly, if the wonderful man had told me to go scuba diving at that stage I would have done it. It was his early detection and thorough care that saved our twins and if he told me it was safe to get up for the last month, then it was time to buy some shoes for the fat-footed.

By this stage I was huge – and uncomfortable. All pregnant women think they are bigger than anyone else has ever been. I found great comfort from long luxurious baths. Bubbles and books, I knew, would be in short supply over the next few years, so I wallowed for hours on end.

It is very common to feel quite isolated as a mother of twins, even before they arrive, so I decided quite early in those months of waiting that I would try and write a book about it, the kind of book I wish I had had to read in the bath back then!

Of course, during the first year very few words were written but when, with Gina's guidance, I began to see the light at the end of the tunnel I got back to the project.

Gina's methods were so effective for our family that I suggested to her that we try a joint project. Could we combine the wonderful *Contented Little Baby* routines with my experience of having twins and following her advice? She agreed and here it is!

I hope it gives every parent of twins confidence and hope. The first few months are exhausting without a doubt. But with Gina's routines life with your babies can quickly take shape. Phoebe and Dora have just turned three and are still napping and snacking the Gina way . . . and yes, it is possible to have a very contented (albeit very messy) house with twins!

Alice Beer

Preparing for twins

1

'Expect the unexpected' – Alice

Trying to give a parent who is expecting twins any kind of advice on how to prepare for their babies' arrival is a hopeless task. I suppose you could start a sleep-deprivation training programme early in pregnancy, or ask a friendly burglar to pop by every afternoon and trash the house, or, better still, you could attach bulky weights to each arm as you go about your daily tasks.

My partner, Paul, and I had different approaches. From my position of enforced horizontal stillness I read every pregnancy book I could lay my hands on. Paul was in denial and read the introduction to the Boots catalogue. Neither of us attended a single antenatal class. I am glad we could not know the way our lives would change when Phoebe and Dora arrived. Equally, without being able to anticipate the love we would feel for them and the thrill they would give us, there is a danger we would have explored the world of contraception a little further!

You cannot prepare for being terminally tired or never finishing a 'To Do' list ever again, so the best advice I can offer you, as a mother expecting twins, is that you swiftly crown yourself the Queen of Organisation. For one thing is certain: organising the complexities of family life will fall on your shoulders. If you are a mother having to cope with limited resources and not a jot of help, you will have to be organised just to stop yourself drowning in the washing, feeding and sleeping cycles. And even if you have pots of money and a house full of staff, the organisation of your domestic empire will still be down to you.

During our preparation time, we discovered that there were two principal things for us to work out, and neither was straightforward: what equipment to buy and what help to hire. Since we were camping in a tiny townhouse while builders sat and smoked in our real home, it was not so much a matter of what equipment we needed, but what we could fit in the space. Our first decision was to get Moses baskets for the early months, as there simply wasn't enough room for cots. What could possibly be complicated about buying two straw baskets with handles? Well, the huge number of different types for a start. Time and again Paul would trot back to my bedside bewildered, with not a carrier bag in sight.

Eventually we acquired the Moses baskets and they proved to be a surprisingly versatile and useful investment. They fitted neatly alongside our bed, one in front of the other, and also on the back shelf of the car on the rare occasions we left the house to visit friends (although not with the babies in them, of course). The baskets sat on the bed while I got sorted in the morning, and they came downstairs for daytime visitors, which meant I had neither to wake the babies nor take coachloads of 'viewers' upstairs. It also meant that if one baby was yelling while the other was sleeping, we could easily separate them. The twins were out of them by the time they were four months old, but I expect the girls' dolls will find them every bit as serviceable.

Jumping ahead a little, peace, quiet and moments of repose come in the form of a place to put your babies where they are stimulated, safe and comfortable. The baby gym is good for one baby at a time, but early jealousy can develop in the spectator stuck with a soft book. (And I think early on Phoebe developed her mother's indifference to the word 'gym'.) I then decided that a playpen was the way to go, and started designing one. I bought two metal hexagonal playpens and created a huge rectangle made up of different areas, some with soft books and others with noisy toys hanging on the sides. It became a haven when the girls were niggling each other, or when the doorbell rang. Later it became a safe place to shut the door on them for the moments when I would reach fever pitch. The playpen lasted for nearly 18 months, which made it worth the effort and justifiable in terms of expense, and it is certainly something I would recommend thinking about sooner rather than later.

In general, as far as equipment was concerned, I decided to adopt a 'How much should I spend on this piece of kit?' policy. I worked out how long things were going to be used for and on that basis slid up and down the price scale. Decent buggies, baby monitors, high chairs and travel cots are worth mortgaging the house for. Other items simply have to work, and frankly a cheap kettle (you will need two) will boil water in much the same way as an expensive one.

As far as clothes were concerned, I followed the fairly standard lists of items printed in all the baby books and magazines. Hats in different colours or with different symbols proved to be a useful identification tool in the early weeks. But when it came to buggies and bouncy chairs, I had no idea what I needed. Much of the time in the early months was spent moving the babies from one place to another, so buggies and car seats became more important than handbags – in fact they are just different versions of handbags. Paul might say that any handbag obsession of mine in a previous single life had been replaced and equalled by my passion for the perfect buggy or car seat – in the right colours, of course!

I was really lucky that a company, on hearing I was expecting twins, sent me two gorgeous bouncy chairs. These were invaluable and I would definitely recommend buying two if you can. Choose a style that can adjust from sitting to lying for the sake of those tiny spines and a little variety.

Since finding out we were expecting twins three years ago, I have found that the most demanding decision was not what to call the babies or how to bring them up, but what buggy to buy. Your buggy is your soulmate for the first four years, so choose wisely. You need to know how wide it is and, importantly, the width of the doorways where you want to go. If your corner store and coffee shop have double doors, you can relax – if not, you will need to find a buggy with a width of 75cm (30 inches) or less, otherwise your life could become very lonely. Pneumatic wheels may seem unimportant for newborn multiple babies that collectively weigh less than a couple of bottles of Evian, but by the end of the first year they'll make going up and down kerbs with a couple of robust babies on board much less jarring on your back. In addition, you need room underneath for shopping (mine has it, but you have to be on all fours to get to it) and the buggy must fit into a taxi (I took the buggy and a sales assistant out onto the street and hailed a cab before I handed over the money).

Once you have found your perfect carriage, you then need to find an alternative person to push it. It cannot always be you or you will go slowly crazy. The mother of multiples desperately needs extra help, although in my experience she may be the last person to accept it. I wanted to prove to my babies, my family and myself that I could cope and do it all. But it really is too much, and even if you are not planning on going back to work, an extra pair of hands will save your sanity.

A partner on paternity leave is wonderful, but not the long-term answer. I think at least one of you needs to get out and see daylight and grown-ups each day. Unless you are lucky enough to have six members of your extended family living in the same street and all desperate to help, you will have the arduous and emotive task of finding someone trustworthy to look after your babies. Many parents cannot afford the luxury of a full-time nanny or au pair, but even a babysitter for an hour or two a week can make a huge difference. Any break is better than none.

A maternity nurse was the luxury that maintained my sanity in the first four weeks; she came highly recommended by people we knew well, so we had no difficulty with that particular appointment. Also, Paul and I have been extremely lucky in that my parents live only an hour away and would walk over hot coals to come and see their granddaughters at any time of the day or night. We have used and abused them and realise how precious their time is with the girls. I have never worried about the happiness of Phoebe and Dora when they go to visit Grandma and Grandpa, but I have worried about the health and sanity of my parents.

Otherwise, as far as help was concerned, I worked on the assumption that applicants were either psychotic or incompetent unless they could prove otherwise. I am confident that the way I have done things has never jeopardised the security of my girls, but I fear it may have worn me out more than necessary, and certainly driven their father to proclaim 'We need some help around here'. With hindsight, the best way to approach the search for help is not to try, as I did, to find someone with multiple qualifications and wide experience of twins. In simple terms, you just need someone with baby experience who can look after one child at a time. Even an hour a day of just having one baby to play with or bath while the other is having her own special time can make you feel much more relaxed. You learn so much about the baby you are with, and it will give you the right to call up your 'single-baby' friends and say, 'I didn't realise it was so easy with one.'

After interviewing several au pairs without success, we enlisted the help of a woman who had worked for a friend. She was incredibly competent and supported us two days a week for the first 18 months of the girls' lives. Never mind if someone has travelled the world with a family of diplomat's children – capability and common sense are by far the most important attributes.

An organisation called Night Nannies was also a godsend on three desperate occasions. Before we got ourselves into Gina's wonderful routines, sleep was rare and unpredictable, and we were both becoming ill with the lack of it. To have someone arrive with experience and the gift of making babies settle when our anxious and exhausted arms no longer could was such a relief. The night nanny arrived at nine o'clock and left at seven the following morning. After the initial weirdness of welcoming a stranger into our spare bedroom within five minutes of meeting, and the novelty of doing the first hand-over, I realised that I did not have to explain how to use a steriliser or describe how to distinguish between Phoebe and Dora in the wee small hours. By the third visit I was already in my dressing gown when I opened the door, and in bed within 15 minutes of our night nanny arriving. The problem then is that you are just too excited about the prospect of sleep to actually sleep!

The girls were three weeks early, which meant I had successfully stopped them coming out for 37 weeks. My suitcase (filled with completely impractical, floaty white numbers) was packed and the cupboards were overflowing with tiny towelling sleepsuits, but our home and nursery wasn't ready, and we didn't yet have all the equipment we needed. Twins frequently arrive a month early, and often even sooner. With the benefit of hindsight, I would seriously recommend that you get everything prepared and ready two months in advance. This is what Gina suggests, and I wish I had followed her advice a bit more closely. So my final tip on preparing for twins is: don't follow my advice, follow Gina's . . .

~

The nursery

Many parents of singleton babies want them to sleep in the parental room at night. With twins, however, I always advise parents, wherever possible, to have a separate bedroom for the babies. Ideally, this room will also have a spare bed or a sofa bed that can be used by the parent 'on duty'. Feeding twins in the early months (see page 49) really has to be done in shifts with a partner, otherwise you will both end up going without sleep, which can have far-reaching consequences for your mental and physical health, let alone the health of your relationship. Whatever the circumstances, never sleep with your babies in bed; it's all too easy to roll over and cause suffocation.

Of vital importance is having the nursery ready on your return from hospital so that the babies can get used to their own room from day one. If, for the first few weeks, the babies doze on and off during the early part of the evening in car seats, when they are eventually put to sleep by themselves in an unfamiliar dark room they can feel very abandoned.

In order to avoid this unfamiliarity, I would suggest using the nursery for nappy changing and naps from the very beginning. In the evening, after your babies' bath, feed in shifts (see page 49) and settle the babies in the nursery from 7pm to 10pm. The night feeds should also take place in this room so that the parent 'off duty' can get some sleep in their own bedroom. If you get the babies used to their own room from the beginning, they will very quickly enjoy being there and see it as a peaceful haven rather than somewhere unfamiliar or unpleasant.

Carpeting

A fully fitted carpet is preferable to rugs, which have the potential to trip you up when attending to the babies in dim light. Choose a carpet that is treated with a stain-guard, and avoid very dark or bright colours, as they tend to show the dirt more easily.

Chair

In the early days you may spend anything up to between 12 and 16 hours a day feeding your babies. A really sturdy, comfortable chair is an absolute priority. Ideally, a small, two-seater sofa bed is the best choice, as it can be used for both feeding and sleeping in the babies' room. If space is limited, choose a chair with a straight back. It should be wide enough to allow room for you and your babies as they grow, and ideally the arms should be wide enough to support you while breast-feeding. I would resist the temptation to buy a rocking chair, which is often sold as a nursing chair, as it can be dangerous when babies become more mobile and start pulling themselves up by holding on to it. In the early days it can also be tempting to settle your babies by rocking them to sleep, but this is one of the main causes of a baby developing poor sleeping habits.

Changing station

The most practical changing station is a long unit, containing drawers and a cupboard. The top should be long enough to hold both the changing mat and the top-and-tail bowl. The drawers can be used to store nightwear, underwear and muslins, while the cupboard can hold larger items, such as nappy packs.

Cot

Many baby books advise that a cot is not necessary in the early days because babies are happier in a Moses basket or small crib. I am not convinced they are either happier or sleep better in these. Generally, I prefer babies to get used to their big cot from day one but in the case of twins, I would advise you to invest in two Moses baskets and two cots. In the early days you may find that one twin will settle to sleep more easily than the other, so having two baskets allows you to separate the babies if necessary, as Alice did.

There may be a temptation to put the twins together in the same cot or basket, but in my experience this can lead to problems of one baby being disturbed by the other. Dealing with one unsettled baby is exhausting enough, so I would not take the risk of putting the two together and ending up with two unsettled babies. Even if they do settle together well in one cot, you may encounter problems later when they are too big to sleep together, but will not settle because they miss one another.

When choosing cots, it is important to remember that they will be your babies' beds for at least 2–3 years, and they should be sturdy enough to withstand a bouncing toddler (or two). If you have a large room for the nursery, you may choose to buy cot beds, which can be used up to five years of age. However, if space is at a premium, I recommend that you choose two normal-sized cots, which may allow space for a small sofa bed, futon or single bed in the nursery. This will allow one of you to sleep with the babies, should you wish, leaving your bedroom for whichever parent is trying to get a full night's sleep.

For the cot itself, I suggest choosing a design with flat spars instead of round ones, as pressing the head against a round spar could be quite painful for a young baby. Cot bumpers are not advised for babies of less than one year old as they can end up sleeping with their head pressed against them, trapping body heat that would otherwise escape through the top of the head. This increases the risk of overheating, which is thought to be a contributory factor in cot death.

Other points to look for when choosing cots:

- Look for one with two or three different base height levels. In the early days you will be picking your babies up very frequently so you will need to set the cot at a height that minimises the risk of back strain. Later, you can lower it to a height that suits their size.
- Drop-sides should be easy to put up and down without making a noise. Test several times.
- The cot should be large enough to accommodate a two-year-old child comfortably.
- All cots must comply with the recommendations set out by the British Standards Institute, Number BS1753. Spars must be no less than 2.5cm (1 inch) apart and no more than 6cm (2½ inches). When the mattress is at its lowest position, the maximum distance between it and the top of the cot should be no more than 65cm (26 inches). There should be a gap of no more than 4cm (1½ inches) around the edge of the mattress.
- Buy the best possible mattresses that you can afford. I have found that foam tends to sink in the middle within a few months. The type I have found to give the best support for growing babies is a 'natural cotton spring interior' type. All mattresses must comply with BS1877 and BS7177.

Cot bedding

Life will be made easier in the early days if you choose 100 per cent white cotton, as this can be put through a hot wash along with the babies' nightwear. Owing to the risk of overheating or smothering, quilts and duvets are not recommended for babies under one year old. If you want pretty top covers for the cots, make sure that they too are 100 per cent cotton, and not quilted with a nylon filling. If you are handy with a sewing machine, or know someone who is, you can save a considerable amount of money by making flat sheets and draw sheets (see below) out of a large cotton double-bed sheet.

To allow for washing and inevitable accidents, I advise you not to stint on the amount of bedding you buy. You really don't want to be drying off sheets in the middle of the night if one or both babies leaks or possets. I recommend the following as a minimum:

- Six stretch-cotton, fitted bottom sheets. Choose the soft, jersey-type cotton rather than the towelling type, which can very quickly become rough and worn-looking.
- Six flat, smooth, cotton top sheets. Avoid flannelette, which gives off two much fluff for young babies; this can obstruct the nose and cause breathing problems.
- Six cotton, small-weave cellular blankets, plus two wool blankets for very cold nights.
- Twelve flat, smooth cotton pram sheets. These are small sheets used specifically for prams and Moses baskets, but are also ideal as draw sheets, which you should put across the head end of the bottom sheet. This eliminates the need to remake the whole cot in the middle of the night or during naps should one of your babies leak or dribble.

Making up a cot

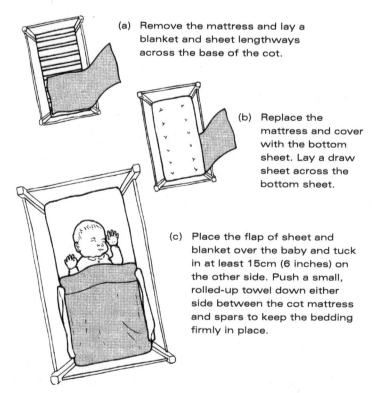

(a) Remove the mattress and lay a blanket and sheet lengthways across the base of the cot.

(b) Replace the mattress and cover with the bottom sheet. Lay a draw sheet across the bottom sheet.

(c) Place the flap of sheet and blanket over the baby and tuck in at least 15cm (6 inches) on the other side. Push a small, rolled-up towel down either side between the cot mattress and spars to keep the bedding firmly in place.

Curtains

The nursery should have full-length curtains that are fully lined with black-out lining (see Useful addresses, page 210). Fix them to a track that fits flush along the top of the window. Ideally, they should have a deep matching pelmet, which is also lined with black-out lining. There should be no gaps between the sides of the curtains and the window frame as even the smallest chink of light can be enough to wake your babies earlier than 7am. For the same reason, curtain poles should be avoided as the light streams through the gap at the top. As your babies get older, they may not settle back to sleep if woken at 5am by early morning sun in the summer, or street lights.

When the lights are off and the curtains are closed, it should be so dark that you are unable to see your partner standing at the other side of the room. Research has also shown that darkness is necessary to alter the chemicals in the brain and condition the body for sleep.

Lighting

If the main light in the nursery is not already fitted with a dimmer switch, it would be worthwhile changing it. In the early days, dimming the lights when settling the babies is a good association signal. If you are on a limited budget, you can instead purchase a plug-in nightlight that fits into any normal 13-amp electrical socket.

Nappy bin

It can be very useful to have a nappy bin in the nursery because of the number of nappies twins generate.

Wardrobe

A fitted wardrobe is a very good investment for your nursery as it enables you to keep the babies' clothes tidy and crease-free, and it will also provide valuable storage space for the many pieces of equipment that you will accumulate. If a fitted wardrobe is out of the question, try to purchase a free-standing version.

Baby equipment

Baby bath

A baby bath is not essential, as babies will outgrow it very quickly. Your newborn babies can be bathed in the hand basin to begin with, or in the family bath using a bath seat designed specifically for tiny babies. There are several types of bath seat that allow your baby to lie supported at an angle, leaving you with both hands free. With twins, my recommendation is to invest in two bath seats. If you would feel more confident bathing your babies separately in a baby bath, I suggest looking for one that fits over your big bath, rather than one on a stand, as filling and emptying is far easier when you have direct access to the bath taps and drain.

Baby chair

While many parents use the car seat in the house for their baby to sit in during the day, if your budget will stretch to it, having a second type of seat for each baby can be a great bonus as it saves having to move seats from room to room – a chore that would be doubled with twins.

Baby seats come in different styles. Some are rigid with adjustable seat positions and a base that can either remain stable or be set to rocking mode. Another type of seat, known as a 'bouncy chair', has a lightweight frame covered in fabric and is designed to bounce as the baby moves. I have found them to be very popular with babies over two months, but they can make tiny babies feel insecure. Whichever type of chair you choose, make sure your baby is securely strapped in and never left unattended. Also, always place the seat on the floor when it is occupied; never be tempted to leave it on a table or worktop as the movement of the baby can easily rock it over the edge. Here are some further guidelines:

- The frame and base should be firm and sturdy with a strong safety strap.
- Choose a chair with an easily removable and washable cover.
- Purchase a head-support cushion for tiny babies.

Baby monitor

This is an important piece of equipment, so don't skimp when buying it. There are generally two types of monitor to choose from – plug-in and mobile – but I would advise you to opt for the mobile version, which allows you to move freely around the house, including areas such as the bathroom, which does not have an electrical socket for the plug-in version. When choosing a baby monitor, look for the following features:

- A visual light display, as well as sound, which allows you to monitor your babies even with the volume turned down.
- Monitors work using radio channels, so choose a model with two channels so that you can switch from one to the other if there is interference, or alternatively, get a digital one.
- A rechargeable monitor is more expensive initially, but the saving on batteries will make it cheaper in the long run.
- A low-battery indicator and an out-of-range indicator are both important.

Baby sling

Some parents swear by this method of carrying a baby around, but others find it too big a strain on their back. With twins it is less of an option, unless there are two of you on an outing, but if you feel that having slings would be a useful alternative at times, here are some tips on choosing the right ones:

- The sling must have safety tabs to ensure it cannot come undone.
- It must provide your baby with enough head and neck support; some come with a detachable cushion that gives extra support for very young babies.
- It should allow the baby to face in or outwards and have a seat with an adjustable height position.
- It should be made of strong, washable fabric with comfortable, padded shoulder straps.
- Try it on in the shop and put one baby into it as one size does not fit all.

Buggy

A double buggy will use up a large part of your budget, so it is essential to choose the right one. First, you need to consider where you live and your lifestyle. For example, if you have to drive to the nearest shops, it is important to choose a buggy that is easy to put up and down, and that is not too heavy to be constantly lifted in and out of the car boot. From personal experience, I have found that tandem buggies, which seat one baby in front of the other, can be harder to push than side-by-side double buggies. However, when choosing the latter, it is important to choose one that will pass easily through single shop doorways. Also think about how the double buggy is likely to perform as your babies grow. For further details on choosing the best buggy, visit the TAMBA website (see page 211).

Whatever type of buggy you choose, you should practise putting it up and down several times in the shop, and lifting it onto a high surface to get an idea of how manageable it is before you purchase. Look out for the following points, too:

- The buggy should be fitted with strong safety straps that go over each baby's shoulders, as well as around the waist.
- There should be an easy-to-operate brake.
- Make sure there is a good-quality rain-hood and apron to protect the babies in bad weather.
- Any extras, such as a rain cover or cosy-toes cover, should be bought at the time of purchase, as designs change frequently and you might not find the right fit later.
- Try pushing the buggy around (preferably with some weight in it) to see how manoeuvrable it is.
- Check that the handle can be adjusted to a comfortable height. This is especially important if you or your partner are particularly tall or small.
- Make sure there's enough storage space.

Car seats

A car seat for each baby should always be used, even on short journeys. Never be tempted to travel holding one of your babies in your arms because in the event of a collision or an emergency stop it would be impossible to keep hold of your baby. Car seats should not be fitted to the front passenger seat if the car has airbags, unless these have been adequately disabled. In general, choose the best seats you can afford, and preferably ones that come with clear fitting instructions. Some shops will advise you and show you how to fit them properly. Other things to look for are:

- A seat with large side-wings, which offer more protection in a side-impact collision.
- A one-pull harness, which will make it much easier to adjust the seat to your baby's clothing.
- A buckle that is easy to open and close, but not easy enough for a child to open.
- Extra accessories, such as a head-support pillow or replacement cover.

Changing mat

You will need at least two changing mats, one for upstairs, one for downstairs. Choose easy-clean plastic with well-padded sides. In the early days it is best to lay a hand towel on the top, as very young babies hate to be laid down on anything cold.

Moses basket

As mentioned earlier, I think two Moses baskets are essential for twins. If you are trying to stick within a budget, I suggest you try to borrow from friends, or buy two second-hand baskets, but remember to replace both mattresses with new ones that comply with the latest safety regulations.

Playpen

Some experts frown upon playpens, believing that they hinder a baby's natural instinct to explore. My own feeling is that, while babies should never be left for long periods in them, playpens can be very useful for ensuring your children are safe while you prepare lunch or answer the door. If you do decide to use a playpen, I recommend getting your babies used to it from a young age. A travel cot can be used as a playpen, but if you have the space, I recommend the square wooden type, which is larger and enables babies to pull themselves up and move around.

Whichever type you choose, make sure it is situated out of reach of hazards, such as radiators, curtains and trailing flexes. Never hang toys on pieces of string or cord in the playpen, as these could prove fatal if one of your babies were to get tangled up. Here are some important points to look for when choosing a playpen:

- Make sure it has a fixed floor so that your babies cannot move it.
- Check that there are no sharp metal hinges or catches on which your babies could harm themselves.

Equipment needed for breast-feeding

Breast pads

In the early days you will use a lot of breast pads, as they need to be changed every time your babies feed. Many mothers prefer the round ones, which are contoured to fit the breasts. You may need to experiment with different brands. Sometimes the more expensive ones offer better absorbency, so can work out cheaper in the long run.

Electric expressing machine

I am convinced that one of the reasons the majority of mothers I advise are successful at breast-feeding is because I encourage the use of an electric expressing machine. In the very early days, when you are producing more milk than your babies may need (especially first thing in the morning), it can be expressed using one of these powerful machines and stored in the fridge or freezer for top-ups later in the day when you are becoming tired and your milk supply may be low. I believe a low milk supply is one of the main reasons why so many babies are restless and will not settle after their bath in the evening. If you want to breast-feed and quickly establish your babies in a routine, an electric breast pump with a double pumping kit will be a big asset. Do not be tempted by one of the smaller hand versions, which can be so inefficient as to put many women off expressing at all.

Feeding bottles

Most breast-feeding counsellors are against newborn babies being given a bottle, even of expressed milk. They claim that it creates nipple confusion, reducing the baby's desire to suck on the breast, leading in turn to poor milk supply and the mother giving up breast-feeding altogether. My own view is that the majority of women give up breast-feeding because they are totally exhausted with demand-feeding, often several times a night. I advise giving babies a bottle of expressed milk from the first week. This one bottle can be given either last thing in the evening or during the night by someone other than the mother, thereby allowing the mother to sleep for several hours at a stretch. This, in turn, is likely to make her more able to cope with breast-feeding. I have never had a problem with a baby rejecting the mother's breast or becoming confused between nipple and teat, but this could happen if, in the early days, a baby is offered more than one bottle a day. Other good reasons for getting your babies used to bottles are:

- It gives you some flexibility.
- The problem of introducing bottles at a later stage to an exclusively breast-fed baby doesn't arise.
- It gives the babies' father a wonderful opportunity to become more involved – and with twins you will need this.

There are many types of bottle available, all claiming to be the best. From experience, I prefer the wide-necked design by Avent, which is easier to clean and fill, and I support their claim that the design of the teat reduces the amount of wind that gets into a baby's stomach. I suggest that you start off by using a slow-flow teat, which will encourage your babies to work as hard when drinking milk from a bottle as when breast-feeding.

Freezer bags

Expressed milk can be stored in the fridge for up to 24 hours, or in the freezer for one month. Specially designed, pre-sterilised bags are an ideal way to store expressed breast milk and are available from chemists or baby departments in large stores.

Nipple cream and sprays

These are designed to care for the breasts and help relieve any pain caused by breast-feeding. The main cause of pain, however, is poor positioning of the baby on the breast. If you experience pain either during or after feeding, it would be wise to consult your health visitor or breast-feeding counsellor for advice before purchasing a cream or spray. No special creams or soaps are recommended when breast-feeding. Simply wash your breasts twice a day with plain water, and after each feed the nipples should be rubbed with a little breast milk and allowed to air-dry.

Nursing bra

A nursing bra has specially designed cups that can be either unhooked or unzipped at the front to make breast-feeding easier. It is important that whatever style of bra you choose fits well. A good nursing bra should preferably be made of cotton for comfort, have wide, adjustable shoulder straps to help support your breasts, and should not press tightly against the nipples as this can be a cause of blocked milk ducts. I suggest buying two before the birth, and if they prove comfortable after your milk has come in, a further two can be purchased.

Nursing pillow

A nursing pillow is shaped to fit around a mother's waist, bringing small babies up to the perfect height for breast-feeding. They can also be used for propping babies up, and make an excellent back support for older babies who are learning to sit up. If you decide to invest in one, make sure it has a removable, machine-washable cover.

Equipment needed for bottle-feeding

Bottle brush

Proper and thorough cleaning of your babies' bottles is of the utmost importance. Try to choose a brush with an extra-long plastic handle, which will allow more force to be put into cleaning the bottles.

Bottle insulator

This is a special type of Thermos that is designed to keep bottles of boiled water warm. It can be very useful when travelling, or for making up night feeds quickly. When buying a bottle insulator, I would also recommend purchasing two small, plastic, three-sectioned containers. Each section can then hold the required amount of formula for three different feeds, which saves time measuring when doing the night feed, and avoids having to carry the tin of formula on days out.

Electric bottle warmer

An electric bottle warmer is not essential, as formula can be heated by standing the bottle in a jug of boiling water. It can, however, be very useful in the nursery for night feeds as it saves having to carry a jug of boiling water from room to room. One design includes a bowl that fits on top, and this can be used for keeping food warm once your babies start on solids.

Feeding bottles

For the reasons already mentioned on page 18, I strongly advise buying wide-necked bottles. If your babies are likely to take all their milk from a bottle, it is important that the risk of developing colic or wind is kept to a minimum. When called upon to help a baby with colic, I often see an immediate improvement simply by switching to a wide-necked bottle. The teat is designed to be flexible, and it allows babies to suckle as they would at the breast. In time, wide-necked bottles can also be adapted to become feeding cups with soft spouts and handles. If your twins are being exclusively bottle-fed you are going to need between 6–8 bottles for each baby, depending on how many times a day you wash and sterilise them. I would advise that you start off with 120ml (4oz) bottles and then progress to 240ml (8oz) bottles.

Kettle

This is essential for making up feeds, so ensure your kettle is efficient and holds sufficient water. A filter for your kettle can also be a good idea.

Steriliser

Whether breast-feeding or bottle-feeding, it is essential that all bottles and expressing equipment be sterilised properly. There are three main methods of sterilisation: boiling equipment for 10 minutes in a large pan; soaking equipment in a sterilising solution for two hours and rinsing with boiling water; or using an electric steam steriliser. From experience, the easiest, fastest and most effective method is the steam steriliser, and it is well worth making this investment. With twins, the number of bottles in use at any one time is considerable, so if you have decided to formula-feed, I recommend that you purchase two sterilisers. It may sound excessive, but it will make your life much easier.

A word of caution – don't be tempted to purchase a microwave steriliser. This type not only holds fewer bottles, but it becomes a complete nuisance when you have to remove it to use the microwave for other purposes.

Teats

Most feeding bottles come with a slow-flow teat designed to meet the needs of newborns. By eight weeks I have found that most babies feed better from a medium-flow teat, so it is worth stocking up on these from the beginning.

Teat brush

Most mothers find that the easiest way to clean a teat is by using their forefinger. However, if you have extra-long nails that could damage the teat, it may be worth investing in one of these brushes, although they too can damage the hole of the teat, resulting in the need to replace the teats more frequently. Short nails are probably the answer.

Washing-up bowl

It is easier to organise and keep track of what is sterilised if all the dirty bottles are washed and sterilised at the same time. You will need somewhere to put the rinsed-out bottles and teats until they are ready to be sterilised, and a large stainless steel or plastic bowl, preferably with a lid, can be used for this purpose.

Clothes for newborns

The range of babywear available in the shops is both delightful and bewildering. While it can be fun choosing garments for your babies, I would urge you to approach it with caution. Newborn babies grow at an alarming rate, and will outgrow most of their first-size clothes by the first month, unless they were very small at birth. Although it is important to have enough clothes to allow for frequent changing, if you have too many, most will never get worn. You will need to renew your babies' wardrobe at least three times during the first year, and even if you stick to the cheaper ranges, it will still be a costly business. I would advise you to buy only the basics before your twins arrive. You may receive clothing as gifts when the babies arrive, and you will have plenty of opportunity for clothes shopping during the first year.

When choosing clothes for the first month, don't be tempted by brightly coloured underwear or sleepwear. Newborn babies have a tendency to leak from both ends, and it is impossible to remove stains by washing at anything less than 60°C (140°F). Brightly coloured garments will soon become faded if washed frequently at this temperature, so stick to white and leave the brighter colours for the outer garments.

In general, keep clothing simple during the first month. Dressing both babies in little white vests and white baby-grows in the early days makes washing so much easier because you can put everything into the same load. If possible, invest in a tumble-drier: it is well worth the expense and means that you do not have to worry about ironing as long as you remove everything from the dryer the minute it is dry.

Listed below is a guide to the basic items you will need for the first couple of months. Until your babies arrive, I would advise against removing packaging or tags so that the items can be exchanged if your babies are either larger or smaller than expected.

Cardigans	4–6	Shawls	2
Day outfits	8–12	Sleepsuits or nightdresses	8–12
Hats	4	Snowsuits (for winter babies)	2
Jackets	2	Socks	4–6 pairs
Mittens	4 pairs	Vests	8–12

Cardigans

If your twins are born in the summer, you could probably get away with just two cardigans per baby, ideally in cotton. With winter twins, it would be best to have at least three cardigans per child, preferably wool. As long as your babies have cotton garments next to their skin, there should be no cause for irritation, and the simpler the design, the better.

Day outfits

During the first couple of months, the easiest thing to dress your babies in will be baby-grows, which usually come in packs of two or three. If possible, try to buy pure cotton and choose a style that opens up either across the back or inside the legs so that you don't need to undress your babies completely at nappy change. Dungaree-style clothes, without feet and with matching T-shirts, are also useful. They will last a bit longer as your babies grow, and the tops can be interchanged if your babies dribble a lot. Choose styles in soft velour rather than stiff cotton or denim for very young babies.

Hats

In the summer it is important to buy two cotton hats with brims to protect your babies' heads and faces from the sun. Ideally, the brim should go right round the back of the head to protect the neck too. Knitted cotton hats are adequate on cooler days in spring and autumn. During the winter, or on very cold days, I suggest a warm wool or fleece hat. Many of these are lined with cotton, but if not, a thin cotton hat can be worn underneath to protect sensitive skin.

Jacket

A lightweight jacket can be useful for babies born at any time of the year. In summer it can be worn on chilly days, and in winter on milder ones. As with other garments, choose ones in a simple design in a washable fabric.

Mittens

Small babies do not like to have their hands covered up as they use them extensively to touch, feel and explore everything with which they have close contact. If, however, your babies have sharp nails or tend to scratch, you could buy the fine cotton mitts made expressly to protect against these things. In very cold weather use woollen or fleece mitts, but remember to put cotton ones underneath if your baby has sensitive skin.

Nightwear

The most common type of sleepwear is an all-in-one suit or baby-grow. This is snug and saves time on laundry, but can be awkward if you have to get your otherwise settled baby out of one to change his nappy. For this reason, some mothers prefer nightdresses. As with vests, 100 per cent cotton is best, and the simpler the design, the better. Avoid anything with ties at the neck, and if there are ties at the bottom, remove them as they could get caught around your baby's feet.

Shawl

I firmly believe that during the first few weeks all babies sleep better when swaddled. Whether you choose a blanket or shawl to swaddle, it should always be made of lightweight pure cotton that has a slight stretch to it. To avoid overheating, always swaddle your babies in a single layer, and when they are sleeping swaddled, reduce the number of blankets on the cot. It is important, however, that by six weeks you start to get your babies used to being half-swaddled – under the arms. Cot-death rates peak between two and four months, and overheating is thought to be a major factor. Always check that you are not putting on too many layers and that the temperature of the room remains between 16 and 20°C (60 and 68°F), as recommended by the Foundation for the Study of Infant Deaths.

How to swaddle your baby

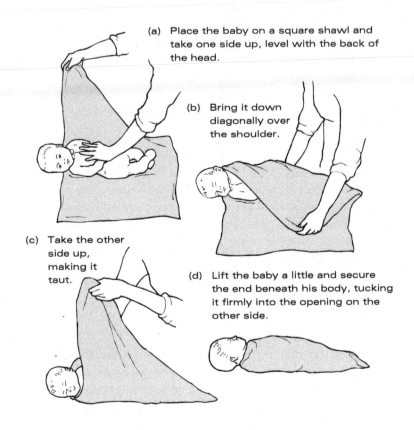

(a) Place the baby on a square shawl and take one side up, level with the back of the head.

(b) Bring it down diagonally over the shoulder.

(c) Take the other side up, making it taut.

(d) Lift the baby a little and secure the end beneath his body, tucking it firmly into the opening on the other side.

Snowsuit

When choosing snowsuits for winter twins, always buy them at least two sizes too big, as this allows plenty of room for growth. Avoid fancy designs with fur around the hood, or dangling toggles, opting instead for one in an easy-care washable fabric. For tiny babies, poppers may be preferable to a zip, which can dig into the chin.

Socks

Simple socks in cotton or wool are the most practical for new babies. Fancy styles with ribbons should be avoided, as should any type of shoe, however cute, as they could harm your babies' soft bones.

Vests

A newborn baby would normally wear a vest both in winter and summer, except in very hot weather. The best fabric next to a baby's skin is 100 per cent cotton, and if you want your beautiful layette to retain its appearance after numerous hot washes, stick to plain white, or white with a pastel pattern. The best style of vest to buy is a 'body suit', which fastens between your baby's legs, has short sleeves and an envelope-style neckline for easy dressing.

After the birth | 2

'Shock or automatic pilot' – Alice

Everyone loves a newborn baby, and interest is more than doubled when you have twins. The world, his wife and even people you've long since knocked off the Christmas card list will all want to come and have a look. My hospital room became just another buzzing Fulham Road location to hang out and drink with friends. Two days after the babies were born by Caesarean, the catheter was out, the stitches were in and I was a wobbly mess coming to terms with two totally dependent, fragile little beings. Around me stood 12 people sipping champagne and passing round my babies like canapés. If I had been in a normal frame of mind, I would have told them all to bog off and leave me alone. But I just took the babies one at a time and sat in a walk-in cupboard behind the reception desk and attempted to breast-feed. That was a big mistake. All those lovely, well-meaning people with generous gifts could have waited two weeks. I wish I had been stronger. Even when you get home, they keep flooding through the door or the doorbell keeps ringing with another delivery. Next time round (joke) I'll make up a medical condition and put them all off.

Paul had decided that two babies and a mother with hands that didn't work properly (as I've mentioned, I had developed carpal tunnel syndrome) justified a maternity nurse. The wonderful Margaret was to stay with us for four weeks, and Paul wasn't going to let me pass through the swing doors of Chelsea & Westminster Hospital until she was firmly installed in our house.

Driving away from the hospital with the babies in the back was the weirdest experience. This was the road we zipped along to go to the shops, pop out for a drink or head to the cinema, and here we were, travelling at five miles an hour in the direction of home with two babies – and we hadn't a clue what we were going to do with them.

It was wonderful taking the babies home – the house was full of pink streamers and helium balloons to welcome us. It was also full of . . . us. We had left the house as a couple on our way out to Sunday lunch with friends and come home a week later with an extra adult and two little pink babies. Rather like my shirts, the house was bursting at the seams. But once we had sat down and had a cup of tea the new order began. The carrier bags stacked in the kitchen with all our exciting new kit were soon ripped open. Nappy bins, bottle warmers and sterilisers were no longer things in a catalogue; they were part of our home and needed to be operated. Paul was a man with a mission: to work out what the buttons did, but the things we most needed instruction booklets for – the babies – didn't seem to have them!

The first seven weeks were just a matter of getting through each day and, more importantly, each night. I didn't move very far from my bedroom or sitting room. It was a claustrophobic period, mentally as well as physically. The minutes and hours just passed in a monotonous round of feeding, changing, dressing and rocking. I had bonded with my babies early, but at this stage (and this continues) they were a business, a challenge and a task. Yes, there were many moments of gazing in total stupor at the little beings we had created, marvelling at their perfection, but it was clear that those special mother/baby one-on-one moments were going to be in short supply.

If I had done the sensible thing and had just one baby, I would have spent the first two months with her strapped to me in a papoose, getting on with things, sleeping when she slept and whipping out a breast at feed times. I still have broody moments thinking about how lovely that would have been. But as my babies lay in their Moses baskets, yelping their little puppy dog cries and waving their arms so vulnerably, I knew we would just have to work it out together. We still are.

I was lucky to have help. Parents of twins need it so ask for it when you do. The babies know their mother, but are too little to care very much if someone else cuddles them for an hour. From the start I found it difficult to hand over the babies. I was exhausted, but if I wasn't with them, I felt like I was missing out. I still do. As I sit here writing this, the nanny that they adore is playing with them downstairs, but I want it to be me who is making them giggle, or thinking of funny ways to make them eat up their tea.

Alice's tip

I found the only help that really worked was out-of-the-house help. In other words, if someone offers you an hour of their time, take it and shove them and the babies out of the house with the pushchair. It is the only way you will sleep or take a bath without dashing downstairs every time you hear a whimper, or, worse still, hear nothing and convince yourself the gas must have been left on and they are nodding off.

With two of them and two of us, it wasn't long before the competitive spirit kicked in between Paul and me. Who could get their baby to take the whole bottle? Bad burping and milk on the muslin definitely earned minus points. Swaddling was another competitive event that they might want to consider for the next Olympics. We believed the tighter the swaddle, the more secure the babies would feel and the longer they were likely to sleep. Well, it became an art form; those poor little mites could barely wiggle a little finger, so determined were we that they would sleep. And if a baby cried in the night and was found to be unwrapped, the parent responsible was deemed a failure.

Most multiple babies will be a little smaller than singletons, some considerably so. Ours were a healthy 2.7kg (6lb) each but still seemed quite little, so the focus of those early days was how much food we could get into them. Every time a poor baby came up for air we would hold the little bottles up to eye level and work out how many millilitres had gone. Paul was always accusing me of tipping the bottle for a better result. With a chest requiring two sports bras and a reinforced vest to contain it, you would think that milk supply would not be an issue. I thought Express Dairies would be calling me. But I underestimated how much tiredness was directly related to milk production. I was exhausted, trying to do too many things at once, so decided not to add another burden by berating myself about continuing to top them up with formula as the hospital had advised me to. Maybe someone will invent a way of telling how much a baby is actually taking when it is breast-feeding; sometimes it felt like pints and at other times I wasn't sure they'd managed even a teaspoonful. I hated not knowing, and often found it easier to express so that I could be sure they had had a good feed.

With those first bottles, the paraphernalia of sterilisers, teats and bottle brushes, along with a whole new dishwasher stacking technique, was bewildering. Eventually it became as natural as washing my face – but lengthier. I soon learnt that everything with twins is time-consuming. There is nothing that can be done quickly, which is totally frustrating for a woman who likes to do 30 things at once to save time.

There were some very special moments in those really early weeks. When the babies were just two weeks old, I had someone come to the house and take plaster casts of their feet and hands. It was such an extravagance at the time, but we are always picking up those little bronzes on our mantelpiece and marvelling at how tiny the girls once were. Having a baby is undoubtedly very special, but there is something very smug about the mother who has just produced two. I can remember feeling overwhelming emotion the first few times we took the babies out in public. Having spent many years on a television screen, I had grown used to people looking twice, but when they took their second and third looks at my little girls I was so proud.

The thing that drove me mad in the early weeks was being completely out of control. The babies, especially Phoebe, would feed in their own time and could not be rushed, so I surrendered myself to their timetable.

I am slightly obsessive–compulsive about timekeeping, and am usually half an hour early for everything. But as we fumbled our way through the first couple of months, we realised that no matter how much time we allowed to prepare, we were precisely one hour late leaving the house every time. It was all just relentless, finishing one task and beginning the next. At first it was all nerve-racking . . . trying to get the little vests on over their vulnerable, wobbling heads, but as they got used to it, so did we. Then it became routine and the obsessive–compulsive part of me kicked in. I would put out two pairs of socks, two hats, two cardigans, two vests, two pairs of trousers, nappies, wet wipes, cream, bottles, formula, scoop to measure formula, bag to keep milk cool, bag to keep milk hot . . . all for a spontaneous trip to the end of the road for a coffee. By the time they were dressed, they were hungry; by the time they were fed, they needed changing; by the time they were changed, they needed bathing; and before I knew it, the daylight was fading and the bewitching hours were upon us.

When I see parents now with new babies I think how easy it looks. In those lovely immobile months, they can't move or break things, empty soap dispensers or cling round your legs as you prepare lunch. Looking back, I wonder why I didn't just sleep or read magazines while they were endlessly napping. You forget about the pumping, the washing, the sterilising and the little cat-like mews that seem at certain times of night and day to be directly connected to your central nervous system.

If you want to do the early days properly, you just cannot have any distractions, but life isn't like that. I found weeks four and five the hardest, when the tiler needed decisions and deliveries of special grout, and the builders turned up each morning expecting me to have somehow magicked up taps and door handles for them to fit. I would feed the babies, then run out of the house to the cheap lighting shop on Shepherds Bush Green, hoping to get back before it was time to pump for the next feed. A particularly good moment was when we moved into the new house: the washing-machine broke down, and for two days there was no running water. Just the time to be captured by a photographer as I was wheeling the babies, steriliser and massive breast pump round to a friend's house to make up the feeds for the next 24 hours. Thank goodness I didn't see the photographer – just his snatched picture in *Now* magazine a little later – or he would have been decked by a large pack of wet wipes.

Parading twins in a buggy with everyone cooing over them is one thing, but being alone with them at night when they are hungry and crying, or wet and crying, or just flipping crying all night long is quite another. I have a few photos of us wheeling the babies around very early on, but I have very little memory of these occasions. In fact, the reason why this book is happening at all is that after seven weeks of fairly relentless demanding babies, I stopped reading *The New Contented Little Baby Book* and started doing it!

~

How will you cope?

I have personally helped look after 16 sets of twins during my career as a maternity nurse, and since retiring, I have gone on to advise hundreds of parents of twins. One of the first questions that each of those mothers asked me is: 'How am I going to cope after the birth?' If you are a pregnant mother reading this book in preparation for your twins, I would like to reassure you that you *will* cope. The majority of first-time mothers have similar feelings of fear and anxiety about how they will manage once they have given birth. The only difference with twins is that those fears and anxieties can be doubled.

Most parents find the thought of leaving the hospital with a baby very daunting. The sudden realisation that they will no longer have the help and support of the nursing staff and that they are now totally responsible for all the needs of their tiny and precious human being can be very overwhelming. Imagine how much more intense that feeling if you have two babies. Between us, and from our different perspectives, Alice and I hope to give you advice that can make the journey of parenting twins a confident and happy one.

The early days

The first and most important piece of advice I can give you about coping in the early days after the birth, and to help eliminate feelings of panic as soon as possible, is the importance of planning your homecoming very carefully. Warn family and friends well in advance that you wish to keep the first couple of weeks as calm and quiet as possible. Learn from Alice and try to keep yourself, the babies and your home a peaceful haven. The outside world can wait a while.

Obviously, a new baby always brings much joy and excitement, and you do not want to deny family and close friends the pleasure of sharing this. With twins this is doubly true. However, it is critical that your babies have time to adjust to their new surroundings. Some can be a little unsettled on leaving the hospital, and this can often be made worse when they are subjected to endless handling, being passed from one person to another. It is also essential that you allow time for you and your partner to get used to having these very special little people in your life, and learn how to meet their many and very different needs. This is difficult to achieve if you have a constant stream of visitors during the first week and the phone never stops ringing.

The calmer and quieter things are, the sooner you will start to feel confident about caring for your babies. In the early days of breast-feeding, tiredness can seriously affect your milk production. Babies are also sensitive to their mother's emotions, and can become very unsettled if they sense you are overtired and stressed.

Twins normally need more sleep during the first month than single babies, but they also need more feeds. Sometimes just an hour elapses between feeding one twin and the other one waking up. It is very important to accept whatever help you can get in the early days. Do not feel guilty about asking relatives and friends to help with shopping or household chores so that you can catch up on extra sleep during the day.

Gina's top tips
- Invest in an answering machine and cordless phone. Train yourself to screen calls and answer only the really important ones. Don't feel you have to chat when you don't have the time or energy.
- View everyone who enters your house as a helper, not a visitor. No one should leave unless they have done something to help, whether it be making a cup of tea, preparing lunch for you or loading the washing-machine.
- When close family and friends come to visit, suggest they take the babies for a short walk while you rest, take a bath or simply have a quiet lunch.

Breast-feeding: what to expect

The second question that every pregnant mother of twins always asks me is equally predictable: 'Is it possible to produce enough milk to feed twins?' The simple answer is 'Yes'. I have advised mothers who have successfully breast-fed twins for up to one year. Of course, in the early days breast-feeding twins is much more exhausting than feeding just one baby, just as caring for two babies is much more exhausting than caring for one. But as

I have already said, getting off to the right start is imperative. This is particularly true of establishing a good milk supply. The key to successfully breast-feeding any baby is to feed little and often in the early days. This is even more important with twins, who usually weigh less at birth. While you will be keen to establish a routine as soon as possible with your babies, do not listen to advice from well-meaning grannies or aunties that they must be kept to a strict four-hourly routine. In my experience, this is the surest way of ending up formula-feeding.

Many babies are unsettled the first few days after they leave the hospital. Dealing with two fretful babies can be very stressful, and suggestions that you are not producing enough milk to satisfy them, or that your milk is of poor quality, will not help your stress levels. This advice, no matter how well intentioned, will also not help you to establish a good milk supply. If you want breast-feeding to be a success, try not to be tempted to start topping up with formula, unless advised to do so by the hospital. This is old-fashioned advice, and the fastest way to end up fully formula-feeding. The exceptions to this rule would be if you suffered a bad delivery and were left feeling very weak, or if you had given birth to a very large baby – unlikely in the case of twins, who are on average 1 kg (2.2 lb) lighter than singleton babies. If you have been recommended to supplement with formula, I would advise you to restrict the formula-feed to the evening when your milk supply is really low. This will ensure that your babies are not crying on and off all evening from hunger, and also allow you time to get some much-needed rest. During the rest of the day I advise that you try to feed your babies from the breast whenever they demand it.

Please remember that *Contented Little Baby* (*CLB*) routines are not about sticking to a strict feeding regime in the early days: they're about structuring feeds so that excessive night-time feeding does not become a habit. Feeding little and often in the early stages is how to achieve this. During the third to fifth day, when your milk comes in, provided you have learnt how to latch your babies to the breast properly, and allow them each enough time to totally empty the breast at each feed, they will not go hungry.

Yes, you may have to feed your babies more often during the first week or so than friends with singleton babies, but it is putting the effort in during those very early days of breast-feeding that determines whether you will successfully breast-feed your twins or not.

If you follow my guidelines for establishing breast-feeding in Chapter 3 (see page 49), along with my routines, you will very quickly build up a good milk supply and have two very contented and well-fed babies, who will start to go for regular intervals between feeds.

Bottle-feeding: what to expect

Breast milk is without doubt the ideal food for all babies. There are so many health benefits to breast-feeding, as I am sure your antenatal classes will already have made you aware. I appreciate that breast-feeding twins may seem a daunting prospect, particularly if you have a toddler or other children already. You might decide that it is not worth even attempting it. I would urge you at least to give it a try. For whatever length of time you breast-feed your babies, it will be of benefit to them, and once you get past those first couple of weeks and see a pattern emerging, it will give you the confidence to continue. Even if you cannot manage to continue breast-feeding at all feeds, a combination of breast and formula is preferable to no breast at all.

In an ideal world, all babies should be breast-fed exclusively for many months, but I realise that for different reasons many mothers are not able to do this. If your own personal circumstances have prevented you from breast-feeding, the important thing is not to feel guilty. Looking after a young baby can be an exhausting business, and looking after two babies is even more so. Please do not waste energy on feeling guilty as it will take away much of the joy that your two beautiful babies will bring you. The most important thing is that your babies are well, thriving and content.

The feeding advice in this book applies to both breast-fed and formula-fed babies, and all the routines can be adapted and adjusted to suit an individual baby's needs.

It is essential to remember that formula-feeding does not guarantee happier, easier infants. Indeed, you may find that your babies go through the same fretful stage on getting home from the hospital as breast-fed babies do. The same advice applies to bottle-feeding as to breast-feeding: please try to keep things as calm and quiet as possible the first two weeks.

If you have decided to formula-feed, I suggest that you discuss with your health visitor which brand is suitable for newborn babies. Formula milk has improved over the years, and now many of the leading brands even produce an organic range.

One advantage of bottle-feeding is that you will be able to see how much your babies are drinking. Provided they get through the required amount of formula at each feed for their weight, they should manage to go three hours between feeds. This time is calculated from the beginning of one feed to the beginning of the next. I would be very cautious about letting your babies go longer than this between feeds during the day. To ensure that they wake for only one feeding during the night, they each need to take the majority of their daily milk requirements between 7am and 11pm. If your babies sleep 5–6 hours between feeds during the day, they would actually be two feeds short by 11pm. They would then probably wake up two or three times in the night to try to satisfy their hunger. When this happens, a mother is often so tired that she allows them to sleep well past the 7am feed in the morning, and a pattern emerges of the babies feeding more in the night than during the day.

During the first few weeks of establishing a bottle-feeding routine, try to stick to the daily recommended amounts for your babies' respective weights, give or take a few grams or ounces. Bottle-fed babies can become quite distracted when feeding, as they have more opportunity to look around, so try to keep feeding time calm and quiet. Do not over-stimulate or talk to them too much as this can cause them to lose interest in the feed. Be guided by each baby as to when he is ready to be burped. If the wind does not come up within a few minutes, leave it and try later. Keep referring to the sections on establishing bottle-feeding and structuring milk feeds in Chapter 6 (see page 107) to make sure you increase the right feeds at the correct times.

Bonding: what to expect

Like many mothers of twins, you might wonder how you can possibly find enough love for two babies at the same time, particularly if you already have a demanding toddler or older children. I urge you not to think about this too much. There will be days when you are struggling to cope with fulfilling their needs and you may wonder if you even like them, let alone love them. But I can assure you that with time you will bond with both your babies. I have seen many mothers of twins trying to meet all their babies' needs all the time, but this is not always possible. You will have to prioritise and meet the important needs in the early days, when they are basically feeding and sleeping, and try to find enough time for special cuddles with each baby. While this is not an easy task, I can assure you that months down the line you will look at your two little babies and feel a surge of love like nothing you could ever imagine.

Each time I looked after a set of twins, I always said that I would never do it again because the first few weeks were so exhausting. But, of course, I did do it again, many times. The simple reason is that there is something magical about caring for two babies; hard work, certainly, but definitely magical too. On down days just keep reminding yourself what I have said – 'Your magical bonding moment will eventually arrive' – and what a moment that will be!

I believe that true bonding is something that evolves over many weeks and months. Whether it is with one baby, twins or even more, do not believe that it is something that all mothers feel instantly. Also, do not be pressurised into believing that 'demand-feeding and sleeping' is the only way to bond with your babies. Mothers can feel depressed, guilty and anxious about not bonding with their babies. The real problem stems not from a lack of bonding but from a lack of sleep. The truth is that for any normal mother, weeks of sleep deprivation, caused by endless middle-of-the-night-feeding, is bound to hamper bonding. That is why both Alice and I would advise you to try, whenever possible, to stick to the routines in this book during the very early days.

Among the many mothers I have worked with and advised, I have found that within a short time of getting the babies into a routine, depression and resentfulness can disappear. It is going to be much easier to bond with two happy, contented babies than two irritable, fretful ones who need constant feeding and rocking.

It is also important to understand that you will feel differently about each baby, and that you should not feel guilty about this. They are both individual human beings in their own right. Do not feel that you have to respond to all their needs in exactly the same way. One baby might like more cuddles than the other; one might yell more when having a bath or nappy change; one might snuggle in to you and feed easily, while the other might fight you every time you try to feed. None of these things makes one baby better or easier than the other – just different.

You may also find that the sleep and feeding needs of twins are slightly different, and this is normal too. The routines in this book will help you to understand what your babies' needs really are, and to know how to fulfil those needs, making the bonding process a happy and more enjoyable one.

Why follow a routine?

As I start to write this section, I can't help looking at the heading and smiling to myself: 'How on earth do parents think they will cope with twins if they don't have a routine?' Of course, I know there are many parents out there who have had twins and coped without a routine. Indeed, many of the twins I personally cared for, and many more that I gave advice on, survived their early days without a routine before their parents called for my help.

But I believe that the early days should not just be about surviving and muddling through, and I have to assume that the reason you bought this book is because you believe that too.

Therefore, perhaps the question should be: 'Why follow *CLB* routines, and why are they so different from others?' I cannot stress enough that there is a huge difference between the old-fashioned four-hourly routines and the *CLB* routines. I could write a whole book on that subject alone. Basically, the *CLB* routines in this book were created to meet the natural sleep and feeding needs of all healthy, normal young babies. They also allow for the fact that some babies need more sleep than others, and that some may be able to go longer between feeds. Unlike the old-fashioned routines developed many years ago, mine do not force a baby to wait for a feed, or become too tired to feed.

The routines are based on my personal work with hundreds of babies, and the success of my advice given to thousands of parents. All settled quickly into a routine, and I made several observations about why they were successful.

Reasons for successful routines

- The parents had a positive approach and tried to keep the first couple of weeks as calm as possible.
- Handling by visitors was kept to a minimum so that the babies felt relaxed and secure in their new surroundings.
- The babies always had regular sleep times in the dark in their nursery.
- They were kept awake for a short spell after the daytime feeds.
- When awake, they were stimulated and played with by the parents.

Those who followed these points bathed their babies at the same time every evening, then fed and settled them in their nursery in the dark by 7pm.

Benefits of successful routines

By following my routines, I would hope that you will soon learn whether your babies are crying from hunger, tiredness or boredom. The fact that you are able to understand their needs and meet them quickly and confidently will leave both you and your babies calm and reassured. The usual situation of fretful baby and fraught mother is avoided.

The other big plus for parents following my routines is that they have free time in the evening to relax and enjoy each other's company. This is usually not possible for parents of demand-fed babies, who seem to be at their most fretful between 6pm and 10pm, and require endless rocking and patting. While twins require a lot more work in the early months, careful planning will allow you to overcome this and the evenings will be yours again within a few months.

Feeding twins in the first year | 3

'Delicate balance' – Alice

No pressure, huh? What about those stories that if you don't breast-feed, your child will get asthma, be stunted physically and intellectually, have a weakened immune system and a million other horrors? And if you do breast-feed twins, the doom-mongers would have you believe that you will be an exhausted, balloon-breasted circus act. In the end, whatever advice comes at you, there are babies to be fed and you just have to get on with it.

About five years before I had my twins I made a film for the BBC about the extraordinary lengths they go to in Brazil to make sure every newborn is given breast milk. Mothers who have extra donate to mothers who don't have enough, and the local firemen go from house to house collecting breast milk to take to the hospitals. I witnessed tiny premature and even orphaned babies being given milk from a central store and realised how important it was.

I took it completely for granted that I would breast-feed my babies. It seemed futile to have carried around a pair of double Ds for so many years without putting them to some practical use. Apart from the huge and much-publicised advantages for the babies, I suspected that it would be a special time. Paul and I were lucky enough to get our family in one hit, so to speak, and I realised that I would have to appreciate all the experiences as they happened because there was not going to be a second time. I knew feeding my babies was one of the most important and womanly things I would ever do, so I was determined to give it my best.

In the months before the girls arrived I was really excited about the whole physical and emotional bonding aspect of feeding them myself. I think most women thrive during pregnancy on seeing the purpose and functionality of their bodies. I couldn't wait to do the most natural thing in the world.

Breast-feeding twins is more a feat than a treat. When my babies were born the hospital immediately offered them a little sip of formula from a cup. That special nuzzling, bonding few minutes that I had been reading about for the previous eight months didn't seem to exist, and I wasn't *compos mentis* enough to protest. I wish now that I had discussed beforehand what happens and what my wishes were. It is so easy to fall into the hospital's routine. The whole feeding scenario was complicated by the carpal tunnel syndrome that had blighted my pregnancy and seized up my wrists. According to everyone even vaguely medical whose opinion I sought, it would disappear soon after the birth, when my body returned to its normal size. Well, two and a half years on and I'm still not 'normal size', so I suppose it wasn't surprising that the pain persisted through the early months. Trying to manoeuvre two babies out of cots and into a finely tuned feeding position was just impossible with hands frozen like claws. I got little sympathy in the hospital; one evening the nurse forgot I was propped up in a chair with both babies latched on. Two hours later, with cramp in every limb, I was still sitting there unable to put the babies down safely. I can tell you that when the poor nurse eventually put her head round the door to ask if I wanted a biscuit, she was told in no uncertain terms what she could do with her custard cream.

Once I got home, I fed the babies together whenever possible. It was just so much quicker, and also the closest I could get to replicating our little pregnancy threesome. Feeding them together was a little like getting Edward Scissorhands to thread a needle, but I persevered. With my impaired manual dexterity, making the fine adjustments so that their tiny faces were at just the right angle was really hard ... plus my breasts were so huge that I had to keep a finger free to make sure their little nostrils were still free to inhale. I worked out a system of rolled up socks, scarves and jumpers that I could wedge around each baby so they were supported in exactly the right position. Those pictures of a smiling woman with two babies happily feeding on a v-shaped pillow are, in my experience, baloney.

I didn't really have any logical plan for increasing the milk supply, but I did notice that it was directly related to how much sleep I was getting. Ironically, I ended up with churns of the stuff when I went filming in Devon for two days. It was ridiculous having to express in the back of a car in Torquay's main car park. I suddenly had so much milk that I was in agony. I thought I would explode as I interviewed Paul Young on the back of a boat. My little yellow travel pump was so noisy that I often wondered what fellow guests thought I was up to in my hotel room in the small hours of the morning.

But there was also something incredibly special about feeding one at a time. I would scoop a little bundle up and have an uninterrupted 10 minutes before another pair of pink fists would start waving around. Then there would be a little overlap until number one dozed off and there was time for some whispering with number two.

Most new mothers will probably invest in a breast pump, which is a pretty bizarre contraption. But when you get into the double breast pump – 'available from specialist stores only' – you are talking about something akin to Sizewell on your bedside table. From day one if I wasn't feeding, I was pumping, and if I wasn't pumping, it was simply because the pump had stopped working or I was mixing formula. Those little mites can sure put away some milk! I can't imagine the dynamics of our little family if I had managed to feed them both exclusively on the breast for those early months. The occasional bottle-feed allowed Paul to be closely involved in the nurturing process, and my parents (still on call night and day for the needs of their precious granddaughters) loved feeding them too. Apart from taking the pressure off us in those early weeks, I think the bottle built important silent bonds between my little girls and the important people who fed them and gazed into their eyes for so many hours.

In the first weeks my maternity nurse was very gentle in advising me to keep expressing little and often to get my milk supply going, and she should probably have been more forceful. I found it hard in the short breaks between feeding armfuls of babies to attach myself to a pump, which was noisy and uncomfortable. I just wanted to sleep or have a grown-up conversation without the whirring noise in the background.

As for bonding while breast-feeding, I have some very special memories of Dora snuggling up to me for a feed in the night when I just lay on my side and looked at her. My little Phoebe found the procedure trickier and had to have bottles in the night to make sure she was getting enough to help clear up her jaundice.

While I am very glad I persevered with breast-feeding, I found it complicated, time-consuming and, in the early days, never-ending. I managed to breast-feed for the first five months, but had to supplement with formula from quite early on. If I had rested more and made fewer calls to builders, I would probably have had a better milk supply, but I did my best. Towards the end I started frantically filling the freezer with little bags of supplies. Every time Paul went searching for the petit pois, he would have to wade through 'October – 3oz' or 'November – 6oz', which I suspect did nothing for his appetite. In the weeks after weaning, whenever one of the girls got a cold or infection, I pulled out these supplies and served them up like some magic healing potion. I don't know if there was any benefit in this, but it made me feel better.

In my keenness to do everything the very best way, I became completely obsessed with the minutiae of how other people were stacking the bottles, teats, rings and tops in the steriliser. I introduced military precision to my kitchen, correcting and berating people for 'not doing it properly'. I sterilised everything – even the knives used for levelling off the powdered formula. And when there was nothing left to sterilise, I descaled the steriliser and the bottle warmer. I think this was my way of staying in control, but there was just so much to do. It was constant and relentless.

Alice's tip

If you are formula feeding an extra kettle is essential – otherwise you will be cooling down the water for the babies' bottles when somebody will come along and make a cup of coffee. They will tip your 'nearly at exactly the right temperature for mixing formula' water down the plughole and you are back to square one and half an hour behind schedule.

Looking back, I realised that before I had a feeding routine, I kept losing track of how much each baby had eaten. Initially, if the nurses in the hospital did a night feed for me and then changed shift, there would be no record of when or how much the girls had taken. It was not surprising that they both lost a little too much weight and took a while to catch up. After a few weeks at home I realised that each baby needed a notebook, or column in a notebook, recording exactly how much she had taken. Here I was Gina Ford-ing myself without even realising it! And coming to the conclusion that if the babies had enough during the day, they would need less at night. It ain't rocket science, but it takes a while to realise this unless you get your copy of *The New Contented Little Baby Book* before the event.

It's ironic really that a woman who had spent eight months constantly eating and a man who had been solely responsible for running up and down stairs with plates hadn't even heard of the phrase 'feeding on demand'. As our gorgeous maternity nurse cradled us through the first four weeks, I just assumed that whenever the babies cried for food it was my duty to supply it. I suppose there was some form of a routine, but they were feeding so frequently, and we were so exhausted and shocked by the change in our lives, that it just seemed completely out of control. We didn't moan too much at first because we'd heard so many dreadful stories about babies being sickly and not eating that we were grateful to have our healthy little girls.

When the maternity nurse left, the days and nights just seemed to roll into one. The walls of our tiny rented house seemed to be closing in on us, so we decided (foolishly) to move back into our own home. Except it wasn't a home – it was a building site. There were no stairs down to the kitchen, hundreds of packing cases, and 10 Polish builders. I exchanged claustrophobia in the rented house for solitary confinement in the new one. The only dust-free room was where the babies slept.

During this time I achieved a new record – not one I'm particularly proud of – namely, five days without a shower. It's probably just as well that I didn't leave the house much. One particularly miserable night Paul went out for a 'really important business dinner', leaving me in the girls' bedroom with no cash for a pizza, the microwave boxed up and unidentifiable, and not even a glass of wine in sight. I had a good old sob and was still deep in self-pity when he came home smelling of the River Cafe's very best garlic.

The lowest point we reached was at seven weeks. Bathed, fed, massaged with expensive oils and swaddled to perfection, there were two babies that, according to the book, should have been sleeping. The problem was that we weren't really doing the book. Six o'clock became the bewitching hour: they would cry and cry and cry – horrible, inconsolable crying – both of them. We tried gripe water in the milk, Infacol in the mouth, back massage, jigging, rocking, pushing and bouncing. Reprieve eventually came about two hours later, when they would gradually doze off on our shoulders as we pushed forks around plates. It was a miserable time, not helped by the fact that there were 52 packing cases in the sitting room, only a microwave in the kitchen and no washing-machine for a fortnight. It was a claustrophobic, noisy, exhausting nightmare.

It was time to take radical action. First, we shouted at the builders. I bet they dreaded going to work each day with a hormonal woman trapped upstairs with two screaming babies. Then I got out *The New Contented Little Baby Book* and started working out how to do things better.

Whether your babies are breast-fed or bottle-fed, it still takes time and perseverance to establish a routine, as we discovered. A bottle-fed baby needs as much guidance and help into a routine as a breast-fed one, the only difference being that the responsibility for giving feeds can be shared rather than falling totally on the mother. This is where Gina's breast-feeding routines can give the best of both worlds to mothers who wish to breast-feed but also want to be able to accept help from husband, family or friends.

~

Guidelines for successfully breast-feeding twins

As you will have read in Alice's account of breast-feeding, she was producing an abundance of milk in the early days and managed to continue for five months with only a small amount of supplementary formula-feeding. Given her special circumstances (the carpal tunnel syndrome and the builders), it is incredible that she achieved this; many women would simply have given up. But she realised that even if her babies received her breast milk from a bottle, it was of huge benefit, and by doing so she managed to provide them with breast milk for much longer than if she had taken the narrow view that it was all breast or nothing.

One of the main reasons that this book came about was because Alice was determined that new mothers of twins should avoid some of the pitfalls that she had to endure in the early days. On discussing her experience, we both agreed that she had been producing enough milk in the early days, and that had she realised the importance of properly structuring the feeds, some of the evening crying of overtired, hungry babies could have been avoided.

This is a problem that I have often had to deal with when advising mothers of twins. I know from experience that those who follow my guidelines from early on report that a definite pattern of sleeping and feeding emerges within two weeks, the babies' weight gain is good and, most importantly, the babies are happy and content. There are, of course, other reasons why breast-feeding can go wrong. I have found that women who attempt to follow the old-fashioned advice of feeding four-hourly can have as many problems as those who feed on demand. Below is a brief summary of how these different approaches can, for some mothers, cause problems with establishing breast-feeding.

Strict four-hourly feeding

In the past, women stayed in the maternity unit for 10–14 days after giving birth. The babies were brought to their mothers for feeding every four hours, allowed a strict 10–15 minutes on each breast, and then taken back to the nursery. If a baby could not manage to go four hours between feeds, the mother was told she was not producing enough milk to feed her baby, and was advised to top up with formula. Such rigid routines meant that it was not uncommon for the mother's milk to dry up long before she left the hospital.

Why strict four-hourly feeding can fail

- Six feeds a day in the early days are often not enough to stimulate a good milk supply.
- Babies need to feed little and often in the early days, so restricting feeding to six feeds may lead to them being short of their daily intake.
- Babies aged 1–6 weeks usually need at least 30 minutes to reach the hind milk which is higher in fat content than fore milk, see page 57.

Demand-feeding

The advice given nowadays is to feed your baby on demand. Mothers are encouraged to let their babies take the lead, allowing them to feed as often and for as long as they want. My main objection to demand-feeding is that very many newborn babies simply do not demand to be fed. This is particularly true of low-birth-weight babies and twins.

The production of breast milk works on a supply and demand basis, so babies who are allowed to sleep for long periods between feeds are not put to the breast often enough in a 24-hour period to signal the breasts to make enough milk. Mothers are lulled into a false sense of security that they have a baby who is easy and sleeps well. In fact, what they have is a very sleepy baby, who, about 2–3 weeks down the line, will start waking up more often and demanding more milk than the mother is producing. A pattern quickly emerges of the baby having to feed every couple of hours, day and night, in order to have its daily nutritional needs met.

The current advice from many child care experts is that this pattern is normal and that the baby will sort itself out, but mothers are not told that some babies can take months to do so. Sometimes a pattern occurs where the baby will go longer between feeds, but this is often one where the baby is feeding so much in the night that when he does wake up for feeds during the day, they tend to be short and small. This leads to a vicious circle of the baby needing to feed more in the night to satisfy its daily needs. The mother then becomes exhausted from several night-time wakings and not enough rest during the day. This exhaustion can often lead to some, or all, of the following problems:

- Exhaustion and stress reduce the mother's milk supply, increasing the baby's need to feed little and often.
- Babies who continue to feed 10–12 times a day after the first week often become so exhausted from lack of quality sleep that they feed for shorter and shorter periods at each feed.
- Exhaustion can make the mother unable to concentrate on

positioning the baby correctly on the breast for any length of time. This means that the baby may not be able to take in enough milk.

- Poor positioning is the main reason for cracked and bleeding nipples, which can also impair how well the baby feeds at the breast.
- A sleepy baby left too long between feeds in the early days reduces the mother's chances of building up a good milk supply.

Another reason I am so opposed to the term 'demand-feeding' is that it is often taken too literally. Every time the baby cries, it is fed, and mothers are not taught to look for other reasons why the baby may be crying, such as overstimulation or over-tiredness.

Of course, all babies must be fed if they are hungry, and no baby should be left to cry for a feed or kept to a strict timetable. But in my experience, and if research on sleeping problems in this country is anything to go by, a huge number of demand-fed babies do not automatically fall into a healthy sleeping pattern months down the line. Many continue to wake up and feed little and often long after the time when they are capable of going longer between feeds during the night. Another problem is that babies who continue to feed little and often invariably end up being fed to sleep. This creates a whole other set of problems, where they have learnt the wrong sleep associations and cannot get to sleep without being fed.

Getting off to the right start

All breast-feeding counsellors agree that in order to produce enough milk, it is essential to stimulate the breasts frequently during the early days. Little and often is the best way to establish breast-feeding. It is also very important from day one that you get expert advice from a very experienced breast-feeding counsellor. Whether you feed your babies together or separately will very much depend on how you cope with latching them on. For many women it comes very naturally, and feeding both babies at once works well. If it works for you, that's great, as it will cut down the length of time you spend feeding two babies. However, not all women with twins can cope with feeding both at once. If you find it proves too stressful, it is pointless to persevere because you will probably find that one of the babies wakes up long before the other one looking for a feed, and any time that you have saved by feeding two together will be lost by having to go back and feed the unsettled baby again. It is essential to accept that during the first few weeks after giving birth most of your time will be spent feeding. Feeds will get quicker, so try not to get too despondent about the length of time it's all taking.

Experiment with different positions and using different types of cushion. While a special breast-feeding cushion can work with one baby, you may find, like Alice, that having a variety of different cushions works best for you. Try to relax during feeds, and concentrate on whether the babies are sucking or feeding. There is a difference, and a good breast-feeding counsellor will help you to distinguish. While it is normal for all babies to spend a certain amount of time sucking rather than feeding, it is very important that they do spend enough time actually feeding. Sucking for too long a period can lull a baby into a sleepy state, where he forgets to feed. When this happens you will find that your baby wakes up 30 minutes or so later, screaming for a feed again.

The most important thing you want to achieve in the early days is that your babies feed well, little and often so that your milk supply builds up quickly and that they put on a good weight gain of 180–240g (6–8oz) each week. It is only when they reach a certain weight and can take larger feeds that they have the physical capacity to go for longer stretches in the night. All too often I have seen parents of twins sticking to such strict feeding schedules that their babies' weekly weight gain is too low. This means that although the babies are at an age when experts say they should be able to go longer in the night, they can't.

The following guidelines should help you get off to a good start with breast-feeding, but I strongly recommend that you seek help from a breast-feeding counsellor. Even if things go well in the hospital, it's wise to get in touch with one of your local support groups so that you can arrange a home visit and, if need be, follow-up visits, until you feel totally confident that you are getting the positioning right. Do not be deterred from requesting this help by someone who is not into structured feeding. Remember, the reason you need the counsellor's help is so that she can check visually that you are getting the positioning right. This will play a major part in getting breast-feeding off to the right start.

Tips to establish a good milk supply

- Offer each twin five minutes on each side every three hours, increasing the time by a few minutes each day until the milk comes in. Remember that the three hours is from the beginning of one feed to the beginning of the next.
  Important: If either of your babies demands a feed before the recommended time, you must, of course, offer it. (To establish whether your baby is genuinely crying for food, see Chapter 5, page 98.)
- Somewhere between the third and fifth day your milk will be in and you should have increased each baby's sucking time on the breast to 15–20 minutes, but one or both babies may need to feed for longer. However, do seek advice from your midwife if you find that either baby is feeding for longer than an hour at a feed, and then looking for food within an hour or so. This is probably a sign that he is not latched on properly to the breast.
- During the first few days, between 6am and midnight, wake your babies every three hours and offer them a feed. Of course, you cannot force them to feed, but I strongly advise you to

try to get them to take even a short feed.

- If you are concerned that your babies are going too long between feeds during the day, and showing signs of wanting to feed more in the night, you should seek advice from your midwife or breast-feeding counsellor.

- Waking the babies three-hourly in the first few days for shorter feeds allows your nipples gradually to get used to the babies' sucking. This avoids the nipples becoming too painful or, even worse, cracked and bleeding. It will also help ease the pain of engorgement when the milk comes in.

- Feeding little and often will avoid the babies spending hours sucking on an empty breast trying to satisfy their hunger, which often occurs when a baby is allowed to go longer than three hours between feeds in the first week.

- A newborn baby's tummy is tiny, and his daily needs can only be satisfied by feeding little and often. If you feed your babies three-hourly between 6am and midnight, the feeding-all-night syndrome should never occur. Even very small babies are capable of going for a longer spell between feeds, and following my advice ensures that this will happen at night rather than during the day.

- Successful breast-feeding can only be achieved if a mother feels relaxed and comfortable, and this is impossible if you become exhausted from being awake and feeding all night. Stress and exhaustion in the first few weeks are two of the main reasons why so many mothers give up breast-feeding by the end of the first month.

- Newborn babies do not know the difference between day and night. They will learn to associate daytime with feeding and social activities only if they are not allowed to sleep for long periods between feeds from 7am to 7pm.

Milk production

Milk let-down reflex

The hormones produced during your pregnancy help prepare your breasts for the production of milk. Once your babies are born and put to the breast to suck, a hormone called oxytocin is released from the pituitary gland at the base of your brain, which sends a 'let-down' signal to the breast. The muscles supporting the milk glands contract, and the milk is pushed down the 15 or 20 milk ducts as the baby sucks. Many women feel a slight tingling in the breast and a contracting in the womb when their milk lets down. If you are stressed or tense, oxytocin is not released, making it difficult for your milk to let down. To achieve successful breast-feeding it is therefore essential to feel calm and relaxed. This can be helped by preparing in advance everything needed for a feed. Make sure you are sitting comfortably, with your back straight and the babies well supported. Take time to position each baby correctly on the breast. Pain caused by incorrect positioning affects the release of oxytocin and the let-down reflex too.

Milk composition

The first milk your breasts produce is called colostrum. This is higher in protein and vitamins and lower in carbohydrate and fat than the mature milk that comes in between the third and fifth day. Colostrum also contains some of your antibodies, which will help your babies to resist any infections you may have had. Compared to the mature milk that soon follows, colostrum is much thicker and looks more yellow. By the second to third day the breasts are producing a mixture of colostrum and mature milk. Then, somewhere between the third and fifth day, the breasts become engorged and they will feel very hard, tender and often painful to the touch. This is a sign that the mature milk is fully in. The pain is caused not only by the milk coming in, but also by the enlargement of the milk glands and the increased blood supply to the breasts.

When the milk comes in, it is essential to feed your babies little and often. Not only will it help stimulate a good milk supply, but it will also help relieve the pain of engorgement. During this time it may be difficult for your babies to latch on to the breast, and it may be necessary to express a little milk before feeding. This can be done by placing warm, wet flannels on the breasts and gently squeezing out a little milk by hand.

Mature milk is thinner than colostrum and looks slightly blue in colour. At the beginning of the feed your babies get the fore milk, which is high in volume and low in fat. As the feed progresses, your babies' sucking will slow down and they will pause for longer between sucks. This is a sign that they are reaching the hind milk. Although they get only a small amount of this, it is very important that they are left on the breast long enough to reach it. It is this hind milk that will help your babies to go for longer between feeds.

Tips to encourage quick and easy let-down

These tips will also ensure that your babies get the right balance of fore milk and hind milk.

- Make sure you rest as much as possible between feeds and that you do not go for too long between meals. Also, eat small, healthy snacks between meals.
- Prepare in advance everything needed for a feed. If you are feeding your twins together, you will probably find it easier in the early days to do so in bed. If you are feeding them separately, ensure you have a comfortable chair with arms and a straight back, and perhaps a footstool. Cushions to support both you and the babies, a drink of water and some soothing music will also help towards a relaxing, enjoyable feed for all of you.

- Whether you have decided to feed your babies together or separately, have a bouncy chair at hand for the baby who finishes first, or who is not feeding at the time.
- It is essential to take your time and ensure that the baby you are feeding on the breast is positioned correctly; poor positioning leads to painful and often cracked, bleeding nipples. This can, in turn, affect your let-down and result in a poor feed.
- Always make sure that each baby has completely emptied his or her breast so that they get the high-fat hind milk. (See page 72 for further advice about allocating a breast to each baby.) If you have been feeding them together, you may find that you will have to give each of them a further five or 10 minutes at the breast separately to ensure that they have emptied it properly. I suggest you do this when you change their nappies, either midway or at the end of the feed.
- Once the milk is in and you have built up the time your babies feed from the breast, it is important that they are on the breast long enough to empty it completely and reach the hind milk. Some babies need up to 30 minutes to do this. You can check if they have done so by gently squeezing your nipple between thumb and forefinger to see if there is any milk still in the breast.
- Never, ever allow your babies to suck on an empty breast; this will only lead to very painful nipples.

Gina's top tip
- If you feed your babies three-hourly between 6am and midnight, the feeding-all-night syndrome should never occur. (Remember that the three hours is timed from the beginning of one feed to the beginning of the next.)

Guidelines for expressing milk

In *The New Contented Little Baby Book* I stress how important expressing is in the early days if a routine is to be established. Breast milk is produced on a supply-and-demand basis, and during the very early days most singleton babies will empty the first breast and may take only a small amount from the second breast; this is the time to start expressing extra milk. By doing so at this point, you will be producing more than your babies need, but will be able to meet the increased demands of your babies during their later growth spurts.

By the second week, the majority of mothers will be producing more or less what their babies need at each feed. This is fine if you wish to follow baby-led feeding principles as your babies need more food: you will go back to feeding every couple of hours or whenever your babies show signs of being hungry. However, if you wish to follow a routine and encourage your babies to go longer between feeds as they grow, I believe it is essential that you are able to offer them the extra milk they need the minute they demand it during their growth spurts. By expressing extra milk in the early days, you will always be producing more than your babies need. When the growth spurts occur the routine stays intact because any increased appetite can immediately be satisfied simply by expressing less milk at the early-morning feeds. I also believe that expressing from the very early days can help avoid the problems of a low milk supply.

During the third and fourth weeks the babies will go through a growth spurt and demand more milk. This is where a problem often arises if you are attempting to put your babies into a routine and are not expressing any milk. In order to meet the increased demand for more food, you would probably have to go back to feeding two- or three-hourly and often twice in the night. This feeding pattern is repeated each time the babies go through a growth spurt (roughly every three weeks) and often results in the babies being fed just before sleep time. This can make it even more difficult to get the babies back into the routine.

Of course, I can imagine you thinking: 'Wait a minute – feeding two babies is going to be hard enough. How on earth can I produce enough to feed both, *and* express extra?' Well, I cannot give a guarantee that you personally will be able to achieve this, but I urge you to give it your best shot. I can assure you that I have sat beside many mothers of twins who have successfully expressed 270–300ml (9–10oz) from each breast! Remember, the key to successful breast-feeding is 'supply and demand'. The more your baby demands, the more your breasts will supply – provided, of course, you follow all the other golden rules of breast-feeding (see page 49). You must also remember to eat and rest at regular intervals. Do not see this as indulging yourself – regard it instead as a necessity if breast-feeding is to be successful. Of course, it is impossible to get an eight-hour stretch of sleep in the early days, but every little catnap and snack will help in establishing and sustaining a good milk supply.

If you have previously experienced difficulties with expressing, do not be disheartened the following guidelines, should help make it easier.

Tips for expressing milk

- The best time to express is in the morning, as the breasts are usually fuller. Once your babies have regained their birth weight and are going happily between feeds, you can then start to express a small amount at the morning feeds.

This is easier if done at the beginning of a feed, and, importantly, allows slightly longer for that breast to make more milk for the next feed.

- Start off by expressing around 20–30ml (¾–1oz) before the 6/7am feed and the 10am feed. After three days, if your babies are still going happily between feeds, I suggest that you increase it to 30–60ml (1–2oz). Continue to express this amount for a further six days, then try increasing it to 60–90ml (2–3oz). Do not get too hung up about the exact amounts – just express what you can. By expressing before you feed the babies you can be confident that they will definitely be emptying the breast of the hind milk, which is much more difficult to express if you were to attempt it after they have fed.

- As Alice found, an electric, heavy-duty pumping machine, as used in hospitals, is by far the best way to express milk in the early days. The suction of these machines is designed to simulate a baby's sucking rhythm and thus encourage the milk flow. If you are expressing both breasts at 10pm, it is also worth investing in an attachment that enables both breasts to be expressed at once, thereby reducing the amount of time taken.

- Sometimes the let-down is slower in the evening when the breasts are producing less milk. In this case, a relaxing warm bath or shower will often encourage the milk to flow more easily. Gently massaging the breasts before and during expressing will also help.

- Some mothers find it helpful to look at a picture of their babies while they are expressing; others find it better to watch a favourite television programme or chat to their partner. Experiment with different approaches to see which one works best for you.

Your questions answered

Q I'm almost five months pregnant with my twin girls. How can I prepare myself for their sleeping and feeding routines?

A • Twins are usually born slightly early and are therefore often of a lower weight than a singleton. This means that you could well have them in hospital for a while, where a feeding routine will have been started. It is usually three-hourly in the beginning.

• Feeds are timed from their beginning, so a baby who begins to feed at 7am will require his next feed by 10am. As you will appreciate, feeding twins will take longer if they are fed individually, so your days will be busy. If you are planning to breast-feed, you must rest between every feed and eat well in order to make the best milk supply possible.

• In the early days many mothers find it better to feed one twin at a time, until they and each baby are confident about positioning and latching on. I suggest you ask for a breast-feeding specialist to visit you in hospital to check that both babies are positioned correctly.

• Maternity pillows, usually sold for the later stages of pregnancy, could also be useful after the birth if you decide to feed both babies together. They are extra long and would support two babies, one each side, held in the 'football hold' (see page 72). I have also found a v-shaped pillow invaluable for propping up two babies together.

• If all goes well with both babies, you can try feeding them together, otherwise staggered feeding works for many mums. The first baby begins his feed alone and continues for 15–20 minutes; you then take him off, wind him and begin to wake the second baby. Change the first baby as the second is waking. If the first baby is content to wait for the rest of his feed, let him sit facing you, in his baby chair, while you offer the second breast to the second twin. Once the second twin has had 15–20 minutes, wind and change him, then finish the first twin's feed on the first breast, followed by the second twin's. Building a 20-minute period between each twin's feeding time can help eliminate some of the crying that is inevitable with two small babies. It also means you will be able to bond individually with each baby; this is especially important with identical twins.

- If you begin this method of feeding from the start, when you are feeding the babies every three hours, it will be easier for you to begin getting them into a routine as they gain weight.

- It is vital to keep written records for each baby. Make sure any helpers you have know to do this as it is very easy to lose track of who fell asleep when in the early days. I find it easier to keep two separate logs, one for each baby. Note the time you began each feed, which side and how long it lasted. If bottles are being introduced, write down how much was taken at a feed. Note how long each baby remained awake afterwards, and how and when they settled to sleep. It also helps to keep a note of wet and dirty nappies, as having lots of help can obscure the fact that a problem may be arising.

- Once your health visitor is happy that your baby is feeding well and gaining weight, check whether you can begin to let them sleep a longer stretch in the night.

- When the babies reach 3.2kg (7lb), you can start trying to follow the routines (see page 107). As with mothers of singletons, you may not find everything going to plan to begin with, but you are trying to establish a framework for each day. Keep trying to get the feeding and sleeping times in place. Settling the babies after their bath at 7pm is very important. You will need evenings where you can rest and get an early night if your husband, relatives or helpers take on the 10pm feed. In order for your babies to sleep well at 7pm, they must have awake periods during the day, especially in the afternoon.

- In the early days take all the help you can get, especially if you are recovering from a C-section. Many mothers find it easier to have someone who hands the babies to them and then winds one while the other feeds. As you become more adept at handling two, you will be more able to cope alone, but any money spent on help in the early days will speed your recovery and help you build the best supply of milk you can. If you have relatives on hand, perhaps work out a rota system for them so that they can all feel involved at different times of the day. Helping you out during the times when the babies are awake is as useful as at feeding times.

- Feeding two babies with breast milk is possible, but it is vital you begin to express from the early days. Use a rented, heavy-duty electric pump with a double pumping kit. It is the most effective way of boosting your supply and takes less time. Use the milk expressed early in the day to give the babies a bottle-feed at 10pm. If possible, your partner or other helper should give this feed to allow you time to rest properly before night feeding.

- Depending on the kind of birth you have, and the babies' weights and feeding abilities, you may be advised to introduce formula. If you are managing to feed both babies some of the time, try not to feel guilty about this. It is best if formula is given at the last evening feed rather than as a top-up during the day, as this will help your supply to remain at its best. The most important thing about feeding, however you decide to do it, is that the twins gain weight steadily, which makes it easier to get them into a routine for sleeping.

- Even if your twins are identical, they may have different ways of getting to sleep. One may drop off easily, while the other finds it hard to settle down. Although you must allow for their different personalities, it is important to remain consistent in how you put them down from the beginning. If you have lots of help, it can be tempting to soothe each baby to sleep while holding her. Try to imagine how life will be in two or three months' time when you have little help and neither baby is able to settle herself to sleep. Of course, you will spend time cuddling your babies, but letting them settle by themselves, provided they have fed and winded well, will be invaluable.

- When they are very young the babies may be ready for sleep one or one-and-a-half hours after waking. In time, as they grow, they will be able to remain awake for the two hours mentioned in the routines. Try to keep their daytime sleeps shorter than the night stretches. You may well have to wake them for their next feed during the day when on a three-hour routine, but this will pay off as they gain weight and are able to sleep one longer stretch in the night.

- As one twin may well go through a period of crying while settling and disturb the other, I find it best to have separate cots or Moses baskets so that they can be separated – in different rooms, if necessary. During their times awake I would put them together under a playgym or musical mobile. Once they are more able to settle themselves, they can go back to sharing a room.

Q I have very small breasts and am worried that I may not be able to produce enough milk to satisfy both my babies' needs.

A • Breast size is totally irrelevant when it comes to producing breast milk. Each breast, regardless of shape or size, has 15–20 ducts, each duct with its own cluster of milk-making cells. Milk is made within these cells and pushed down the ducts when the baby sucks. During the early days make sure your babies are put to the breast frequently. Most babies need a minimum of eight feeds a day to help stimulate the breasts and establish a good milk supply.

- Although I recommend that you express only at the beginning of the morning feeds, in the early days you may find that one baby, or even both of them, is not totally emptying the breast at all the feeds. If this is the case, take advantage of expressing a little milk before each feed and freezing it. As mentioned earlier, I think it is better to express at the beginning of the feed, first because it is easier, and second because the babies will reach the hind milk more quickly, and are more efficient at emptying the breast than an electric pump. It is always good to have a supply of frozen breast milk so that you can occasionally leave the babies with someone else for a few hours and get a complete break.

Q Should I feed my babies together or separately? I feel that feeding them together might make them miss out on that individual bonding process. But feeding them separately would take so much longer.

A • There are advantages and disadvantages to both methods. If you can manage to feed your babies together successfully, the time you spend feeding will be slightly shorter. However, this is very dependent on whether the babies feed efficiently.

• If one baby is a slow or sleepy feeder, you could find that he or she does not get enough during the feed and demands to be fed long before the next feed is due. Therefore, in terms of total feeding time, nothing has been saved.

• Feeding them separately does take slightly longer in the early days – possibly around 20–30 minutes a feed – but this does give you enough time to ensure that each baby is fed properly. As they get bigger and feed more quickly, the time spent feeding does reduce. From my personal experience of working with twins, I found that while feeding them individually took longer, it reduced the burden of trying to fulfil the needs of two crying babies at once. I suggest that you experiment with both methods. Try individual feeding for a whole day, then joint feeding the next, and decide which suits you best. With regard to bonding, do remember that feeding is only a part of mothering. As long as you manage to spend a little time alone with each baby every day, you will form a bond with them both.

Q My friend was in agony when her milk came in. Is there anything I can do to help relieve the pain of engorgement?

A • Put your babies to the breast often and do not let them go longer than three hours between feeds in the early days. A warm bath or warm wet flannels placed on the breasts before a feed will help the milk flow, and gently expressing a little milk by hand could make it easier for the baby to latch on. Damp flannels chilled in the fridge and placed on the breasts after a feed will help constrict the blood vessels and reduce the swelling. Similarly, chilled cabbage leaves placed inside your bra between feeds will also help to ease discomfort. Make sure you wear a well-fitting nursing bra that supports your breasts without flattening your nipples, and is not too tight under the arms.

Q Many of my friends have had to give up breast-feeding because it was so painful. Is this likely to happen to me?

A • The main reason women experience pain in the early days is because the baby is not correctly positioned on the breast. He ends up chewing on the end of the nipple, causing much pain for the mother, and the result is often cracked, bleeding nipples and a poor feed for the baby. A pattern soon emerges of the baby needing to feed very quickly again, giving him even more opportunity to damage the nipples. This is why I urge you to seek expert help from a breast-feeding counsellor, particularly if you are planning to feed the babies at the same time for most of the feeds. Trying to position two babies together is a skill that takes some practice, and by getting it right from the very beginning you will avoid the problem of cracked nipples.

• If you decide to feed the babies separately, make sure that you always hold the baby you are feeding with his tummy to your tummy and that his mouth is open wide enough for him to take all the nipple and as much of the areola as he can manage into his mouth. Apart from ensuring that your baby is well positioned, it is important that you are sitting comfortably. The ideal chair should have a straight back, preferably with arms, so that you can position a cushion to support the arm in which you are holding the baby. If you do not support your arm, it will be much more difficult to position and support your baby properly. This can cause him to pull on the breast, which will be painful for you.

Q Do I need to avoid certain foods while breast-feeding?

A • You should continue with the same varied, healthy diet that you followed throughout your pregnancy. In addition, you should include small, healthy snacks between meals to help keep your energy levels up. Ensure that you eat at least 175g (6oz) of poultry, lean meat or fish on a daily basis. Vegetarians should eat the equivalent in beans, pulses and other forms of protein. I have noticed that on the days when some of my breast-feeding mothers did not eat enough protein, their babies were much more unsettled. Some research points to dairy products as the cause of colic in certain babies. If you find your babies develop colic, it may be wise to discuss how to monitor your dairy intake with your health visitor or paediatrician.

• Artificial sweeteners and caffeine should be avoided. Remember that caffeine is found not only in coffee, but also in tea, cola drinks and chocolate. I have noticed that all these things can upset most babies. Strawberries, tomatoes, mushrooms, onions and fruit juice, if taken in large quantities, have left many of my babies very irritable. While I do not suggest cutting out all these things from your diet, I suggest you keep a record of any food or drink consumed 12–16 hours prior to your baby showing signs of tummy ache, explosive bowel movements, excessive wind or crying fits. While working in the Middle and Far East, I observed that breast-feeding mothers followed a much blander diet than normal, and highly spiced foods were omitted. Perhaps it would be wise to avoid curries in the early days.

- Although it is advisable to avoid alcohol, especially spirits, while breast-feeding, some experts advise that a small glass of wine, or a Guinness, can be beneficial to a mother who is finding it hard to unwind in the evening. I suggest you discuss this with your midwife or GP if you are unsure whether you should occasionally indulge or not.

Q I am very worried about the idea of feeding two babies. Is it really possible?

A • Confidence and the feeling that it *is* possible are two of the most important factors in deciding to breast-feed your twins. Breast is best and the most natural way to feed your babies, as all the baby experts agree. Twins are more likely to be born early than single babies, and 40 per cent of twins or triplets require time in special care. If babies are born early, their mother's milk will be different from full-term milk and have specific advantages for pre-term babies. Breast milk reduces a baby's chances of catching infections, some of which can be particularly serious in a pre-term baby.

- If your twins are born very early, they may need to be fed by tube or special cup until they are able to breast-feed. Expressing breast milk for premature babies can help you feel you are making a valuable contribution to your babies' welfare, especially as hospital staff are responsible for other aspects of their care.

Q I am pregnant with twins and already have three children. I want to follow the *CLB* routines as soon as I can with the twins, and have duly hired a breast pump, but am unsure about when to use it. Your book recommends that you express milk in the morning from the breast the baby isn't feeding from, but with twins both breasts will be emptied at each feed. When would you recommend I try to express?

A • Once your babies have regained their birth weight and are happily going three hours from the start of one feed to the next, you can start to express a little before morning feeds (see page 60 for further details). I suggest using the milk you express at these feeds to replace one feed of the day for both babies when things are really hectic with all the other children. Some mothers find that trying to breast-feed twins at 5pm/6.15pm, when other children are demanding attention, can be very difficult.

- By giving expressed milk from a bottle at these feeds, you will know for certain that each baby has had enough to settle, and this will allow you more time to cope with the other children.
- Another point when you could use expressed milk from a bottle is at the 10am feed, if this is a particularly busy time for you. Alternatively, if you have some help, you can alternate the babies' feeds, with one being given the breast and one being given a bottle of expressed milk.
- If you collect milk for the 10pm feed, this could be given as an expressed feed by your partner, thus enabling you to have an early night. If you do decide to do this, express both sides fully before going to bed in order to maintain your supply.
- If you have some help arranged, you should rest as much as possible between feeds, as well as eating healthy food and drinking a lot of fluids. Chances are that everyone will be only too pleased to help you successfully feed both babies. As you fed your other three children, you will know what to expect, but try not to feel guilty if you do find you need to introduce formula at some point. It is better to do this and manage to continue breast-feeding than attempting to do it all and having to give up completely through exhaustion. If you do decide to introduce some formula, I suggest you do so at the evening feeds whenever possible. Formula is digested differently from breast milk, and offering too much at daytime feeds could result in your own milk decreasing too rapidly.

Q My twin boys are 19 weeks old and formula-fed. They have always been quick feeders and had good appetites. Just recently they have started to become fussy, leaving milk at

several feeds each day. I have been trying to get them to take most of their feeds, but they get distressed after a while. I don't want to start snack-feeding them as it will be never-ending. What can I do?

A • It seems that your boys are just not hungry at some feed times, so it is worth stretching them out a little. While two babies mean that you have to begin feeding slightly earlier than with a singleton, leaving them another 15–20 minutes before starting can make a big difference.

• If they have been sleeping well from 10pm to 6.45am, try decreasing the last night-time feed very gradually by 60ml (2oz) over several days and see if they are hungrier at 6.45am. Some babies are able to drop this feed before beginning solids, but the same amount will need to be added to their daily feeds somewhere so that they do not cut back too heavily on their milk intake. If, after doing this, you find they are hungrier at 6.45am, they should be able to take their full feed, or possibly even 240ml (8oz). After a week of increased 6.45am feeding, you could try not waking them at 10pm. Be aware that this may lead to earlier morning waking through hunger – something you may not want to return to.

• Once you begin to wean the boys (on the advice of your health visitor or GP), you will be aiming to push their 10.45am feed later so that it turns into lunch at 11.45/12.00. Begin to delay it a little now by starting their feed at 11am and finishing about 11.30am. Waiting that extra 15 minutes could really help. In turn, this should help them cut back a little at 2.15pm. Taking 180ml (6oz) at this feed should help them to be hungrier at 6pm and more willing to finish their full feed. Later, if possible, you could delay beginning the bath until 5.45pm, and aim to feed them at 6.15/6.30pm so that they are more willing to take a full feed. Some babies of this age are settled between 7 and 7.30pm. As the boys still take a short afternoon nap, try pushing the routine forward by 15 minutes to help them feel hungrier for each feed without getting overtired.

Q Should I alternate breasts when feeding my twins, or should I allow each baby to feed from the same breast at every feed?

A • In my experience, the majority of mothers have one breast that produces more milk than the other, and with most twins one always feeds more than the other. As breast milk is produced on a supply-and-demand basis, I advise you to allow each baby its 'own breast'. This way you can feel confident that each baby's individual needs are being met.

Q I want to try to feed both babies at the same time and have been told that the 'football hold' is the best feeding position for doing this. What is the 'football hold' and does it mean that I am going to have to do all my feeding in bed?

A • The 'football hold' is so called because you hold the babies as if you are a rugby football player holding two balls. Tuck a baby under each arm, using pillows or cushions as supports. The babies should be facing you with their noses level with your nipples. This position is ideal if you've had a C-section as the babies will not be resting on your stomach.

• There are positions other than the football hold which you can discuss with your breast-feeding counsellor. Provided you have a deep sofa or large chair, you should manage, with practice, to feed both babies using your preferred method. Sometimes I have found that twins will feed better if the position is changed midway through the feed or after burping.

• Another option is to feed both babies at the same time for 20 minutes or so, then change their nappies and give each of them an individual feed of a further 10–15 minutes. This method helps ensure that each baby has emptied its own breast well, and still keeps feeding time for both babies to within an hour.

Understanding your babies' sleep | 4

'And trying to get some yourself...' – Alice

We began taking the *CLB* routines seriously when the babies reached about three months of age. Up until then, feeding and sleeping had been a bit of a blur for all of us. I didn't realise how desperate for a routine we actually were. I was carefully monitoring how much milk each of the girls was taking, and also trying to make their feeding and sleep patterns regular and organised, but it wasn't working very well. Looking back, I was trying to write *The New Contented Little Baby Book* by myself, despite the fact that I had a copy in front of me. When the babies took their bottles, I tried to feed them together. In a funny way it seemed quite sociable. I would have them in their bouncy chairs or sitting on the sofa with me, where I would wriggle myself into a position so I could aim a teat into each baby's mouth at the same time. They didn't seem to get cross or fight for prime position this way, whereas every time I tried to feed just one baby it seemed like favouritism and the other looked so hurt – like she was missing out on the fun. I did feel guilty when they were propped up in front of me rather than being held, but sitting facing them gave me lovely eye contact, which I felt was essential.

I soon learnt that any kind of routine with multiples is all about doing it the best way you can. I often found myself giving the 2pm feed at a café in Putney Shopping Centre, with one baby on my lap and one in the pushchair. It relieved the isolation of being at home with them alone, but, despite plenty of practice, it never became easy to simultaneously eat a muffin and feed them both.

Phoebe and Dora have always seemed to do things together, so when they hit three months and should have been starting to settle each night, they were actually both crying constantly from six to nine o'clock each and every evening. It was awful. We tried changing the formula, changing the amounts, changing their nappies and changing their timings. We were desperate. The only thing left for us to change was moving their Moses baskets into rooms at the back of the house because we were mortified about what the neighbours thought.

Before we started taking Gina's routines seriously, night-time feeds really began to get to me. Standing by their cots in the lonely darkness, I felt there was just too much to work out. Phoebe was awake and crying, so should I wake Dora and feed them both at once? Was it worth making that big effort so I got back into bed earlier? Or should I leave Dora until I had finished Phoebe, then wake her and try to feed her when she probably wasn't hungry and just wanted to sleep? Or should I just feed Phoebe, then go back to bed and lie waiting for Dora to cry 10 minutes after I had dozed off? Whichever option I chose, like the supermarket checkout queue, was bound to be the wrong one.

The girls never really seemed to wake each other up, which people are always obsessed about with twins. I was constantly amazed that one would be sleeping while the other cried and wailed impatiently as I fumbled with her bottle.

During those horrid hours, when you don't even want to know what time it is, I vowed I would do two things when my life was more ordered: write a book on bringing up twins, and manufacture a bottle-warmer system for two bottles. Maybe next year I will get onto the second project. We kept the bottle warmer in the babies' bedroom, the theory being that the person 'on duty' could change one nappy while warming up the first bottle, then heat up the second bottle while feeding the first baby. But every single time the milk would overheat, meaning that you would have to steal some from the cold bottle, in the process spilling precious expressed breast milk onto new cream carpets . . . a double whammy. Or the formula, neatly spooned out into the compartmented container, would spill all over the chest of drawers as you tried to wind the first baby while preparing the feed for the second. I didn't often succumb to tears, but I do remember just holding them both on the sofa in their room during a particularly bad night: they wailed and I wept. It sounds strange, but I loved them more than ever at that moment, and when I recall it I just want to go and hug them tight; it was a night when we three girls all needed each other.

From the very beginning we intended that the girls would share a room. I wondered whether I was being unkind putting them in separate Moses baskets after their closeness in the womb, but they seemed to appreciate their own space, while taking comfort in the knowledge that their sister was near.

The girls were always restless at different times, and I think Phoebe would naturally wake earlier than Dora, while Dora would always be last to fall asleep. I am never convinced that sleep patterns are biological: if the members of a family are early risers, it is probably because one is disturbing the others. I suspect that is the way with twins. It sounds like a nightmare but the slight variation in their natural sleep urges helped me to stick to the routines as Phoebe was always, and still is, happiest to go into her cot first. Try putting Dora in first and the whole street will know about it!

The most important thing that following the *CLB* routines taught me was that feeding and sleeping are very closely linked: in order to get sleep right, it is essential to get the feeding right. Also, I realised how much the babies' feeding needs kept changing during the first few months. You no sooner think you've cracked it than you notice things starting to go a bit pear-shaped. I quickly learned that following the routines was not only the key to having two happy, well-rested babies, but it made me aware of sleep rhythms, and this really helped me understand just how the wrong sleeping associations can creep in. With one baby it may be possible for a parent to survive rocking it to sleep, getting up several times a night and to comfort it back to sleep again. But with two babies and two dodgy hands, I knew that it was not even an option I could consider.

The benefit of following the *CLB* routines is not only that you get the feeding times right and ensure a baby takes enough at each feed, but that you come to understand about the natural sleep rhythms of young babies. I went on to read Richard Ferber's *Solve Your Children's Sleep Problems*, and would really recommend it, even though it is often heavy going. That, together with *CLB's* information on creating the right sleep associations, was invaluable.

~

Understanding sleep

I know that one of the questions uppermost in your mind is 'When will my babies sleep through the night?' As sleeping through the night depends on many factors and I do not know your babies personally, I cannot give you a specific answer. What I *can* tell you, however, is that nearly all the twins I have cared for slept through the night between 12 and 16 weeks. This is reinforced by messages posted on my website, which indicate that this is the average age for twins following the *CLB* routines from birth. Twins who have started the routines later will probably take a little longer to sleep through. Whatever the case, it is important to understand that sleeping through the night at this age means from the last feed at 10pm to 6/7am the following morning.

For you to achieve a healthy sleeping pattern for your babies and avoid months of sleepless nights, it is important that you are consistent and persistent with the routines in this book. By being patient and structuring your babies' sleeping and feeding to meet their individual needs, and establishing the right sleep associations, you can achieve this. I am not saying that it will be easy; it will take a lot of determination at times. But the fact that thousands of parents of twins have already achieved this by using *CLB* routines will, I hope, help to reassure you that it is possible.

The golden rule to ensuring a long-term, healthy sleep pattern is the same for twins as it is for one baby. From the day you get home from the hospital you should endeavour to establish the right sleep associations and structure your babies' feeds during the day so that excessive night-time feeding due to hunger never becomes a problem.

As Alice has already said, waking the babies for feeds is one of the hardest parts of the routines – particularly if you are bombarded with well-meaning advice that it is wrong to wake a sleeping baby, and that all babies eventually find their own routine. This may very well be true, but the fact that we have over 120 NHS sleep clinics and hundreds of private ones dealing with the sleeping problems of young babies and toddlers is proof that a huge number are not sleeping well at night.

Sleep and demand-feeding

Some advocates of demand-feeding believe that following a routine is about denying young babies food when they are hungry in order to regulate their feeding and force them to sleep through the night. While this may have been true of old-fashioned four-hourly feeding schedules, it is not true of *CLB* routines. In fact, my experience of working with many premature babies and sets of twins went a long way towards helping me develop the routines. I observed that these small babies were always woken for feeds. The hospital staff would not have dared to allow them to go too long between feeds as the lives of these tiny, sleepy babies depended on being fed little and often. When the mothers and babies were eventually discharged from the maternity unit, a three-hourly feeding routine was usually in place.

I imagine that the staff in the maternity unit where you give birth would also advise you to feed regularly. If they are advocating that your babies are left for longer than three hours between feeds, I suggest that you ask their reasons for this, particularly if you find that your babies are sleeping four or five hours between feeds during the day, and then waking up every two hours in the night.

If you read books about breast-feeding, you will see that they nearly all say it is normal for newborn babies to need as many as 8–12 feeds a day. You do not need a degree in maths to work out that a baby who has had only three or four feeds between 6am and 6pm will have to feed on and off all evening and during the night to satisfy his needs. A vicious circle soon evolves where the baby is awake and feeding on and off during the night, and is so tired that he cannot be woken for feeds during the day.

Many experts believe that this is a normal pattern that will eventually sort itself out, and they advise that the mother should rest during the day while the baby sleeps. This advice may well work for a mother of a first baby, who is not too concerned about connecting with her husband or the outside world for weeks and perhaps months. But parents with older children quickly realise that demand-feeding is usually quite unrealistic. You will already understand that in order to cope, you will have to wake the babies in the morning so that you can fit in everyone's needs. If you are a first-time mother of twins, I would stress that you should not allow anyone to make you feel guilty about waking your babies for feeds. Hundreds of thousands of parents are doing the same thing every day and have very happy, contented babies who sleep and feed well. Remember, one of the main aims of the *CLB* routines is that you meet your babies' needs before things reach a stage where they have to cry to have them met.

As Alice has written, things started to get better for her with Phoebe and Dora when she began structuring their feeds more and got better at understanding their sleep rhythms. The routines will also be easier for you to understand and follow if you have some knowledge of sleep rhythms. Taking the time to read and understand some basic information will help you adapt the routines to suit the individual needs of your babies, and encourage them to sleep through the night as soon as they are physically able to do so. An understanding of sleep rhythms will also help you to adjust the routines on occasions when it is not always possible to follow them to the letter.

Sleep rhythms

A newborn baby will sleep approximately 16 hours a day in the first few weeks. If your twins have been born early, as many are, they will probably sleep a little more than this each day. Sleep in the early days is closely linked to the baby's need to feed little and often. It can take well up to an hour to feed, burp and change each baby, after which they fall quickly into a deep sleep, often sleeping through to the next feed. Over a 24-hour period, with an average of 6–8 feeds a day lasting between 45 minutes and one hour, the baby ends up sleeping approximately 16–18 hours a day.

Usually between the third and fourth week most singleton babies become more alert and will not fall straight into a deep sleep after feeding. If your babies were born slightly early, this may happen between their fourth and sixth week.

It is around this time that the different stages of sleep become more apparent. Like adults, babies drift from light sleep into a dream-like sleep known as REM (Rapid Eye Movement) sleep, then into a deep sleep. The cycle is much shorter than that of an adult, lasting approximately 45 minutes to one hour. While some babies stir only when they drift into light sleep, others will wake up fully. If the baby is due for a feed, this does not create a problem. However, if it is only one hour since the baby fed and he does not learn to settle himself, a real problem can develop over the months ahead.

Recent research has shown that all babies drift into light sleep and wake up approximately the same number of times during the night. Only the poor sleepers are unable to drift back into deep sleep, and this is because they are used to being helped to sleep.

If you want your babies to develop good sleep habits from an early age, it is important to avoid the wrong sleep associations.

The bedtime routine

Once your babies have regained their birth weight and are regularly putting on at least 180–240g (6–8oz) each week, you can look at establishing a regular bedtime of 6.30/7pm, allowing them to sleep past the 9pm feeding, and feed them around 10pm. It is at this stage that they should manage to go slightly longer in the night. If they both take a good feed at 10/10.30pm and you settle them between 11/11.30pm, they should manage to sleep until between 2/3am. If they are both properly awake and feed well then, and settle back within an hour, they should hopefully get through to around 6/7am.

Establishing a good bedtime routine and getting your babies to sleep well between 7pm and 10pm is a major factor in how quickly they will sleep through the night. A baby who feeds well at 6pm and settles to sleep well between 7pm and 10pm will wake up refreshed and ready to take a full feed. However, there are other factors in establishing a regular bedtime routine. The main one is that you have structured your babies' feeding and sleeping pattern during the day so that they are hungry enough to take a full feed at 5/6.15pm, and have been awake enough during the day that they are ready to sleep.

I get many calls from parents struggling to establish a bed-time routine and settle their babies in the evening. When a pattern of feeding on and off occurs during the early evening, it has a knock-on effect of the babies not being hungry enough at the 10pm feed, and then waking several times during the night genuinely hungry.

Whether you have one baby or two, or even more, the key to encouraging good sleep at night is dependent on what you do during the day. Once your babies are gaining a regular weight of at least 180–240g (6–8oz) each week, it means they are growing well. As they grow, the amount that they can take at each feed should increase, and they should gradually be able to go longer between feeds. This will not necessarily happen automatically, and it brings us back to what you may find the hardest part of the routines – the need to wake your babies for daytime feeds. But if you think about it logically, I am sure you will agree that it makes sense for babies who have fed regularly during the day to need less feeding in the night. In order for any baby to sleep through the night, it must have all its nutritional needs met during the day. Try, whenever possible, to stick to the recommended times that I advise in the routines and ensure that your babies take a full feed at those times. Also make sure they are awake for short spells after the daytime feeds.

In the early days start the bedtime routine no later than 5.30pm. If your babies have not slept well at nap times, you may need to start earlier. Try to keep things very calm and quiet throughout the bath, and afterwards avoid lots of eye contact and talking so that the babies do not become overstimulated. Always try to do the last part of the feed in the nursery, keeping it dimly lit so that you can quickly settle each twin in his cot before he falls asleep. It will be hard work, but believe me, the effort you put in during these early weeks will be well rewarded when your babies happily start to go longer and longer in the night, until they eventually make it through to that magical time of 6.45am.

Early-morning waking

Whether a child becomes an early-morning waker is largely determined by what happens during his first year. In order to avoid this problem, it is crucial that your twins sleep in a very dark room and that the mother treats any feeds before 6.45am as night-time feeds. They should be done with the minimum of fuss, no talking or eye contact, and the babies should be settled back to sleep until 7.30am. Of course, some older babies do wake up around 5/6am, and perhaps chatter or sing for a short spell, but they eventually return to sleep.

Somewhere between eight and 12 weeks the majority of babies do not wake up from naps immediately looking for food. This is a good time to encourage them to lie in their cot for a short while after waking. By doing this, and following the guidelines below, there will be less chance of your baby becoming an early-morning waker.

- Research shows that the chemicals in the brain work differently in the dark, preparing it for sleep. Get your babies used to sleeping in a very dark room with the door shut from day one. Even the smallest amount of light can be enough to wake a baby fully when he comes into a light sleep.
- Until the age of six months the 'Moro reflex', in which the baby flings his arms and legs back in jerky movements, can be quite strong. It tends to happen if he is startled – perhaps by a sudden loud noise, or being put down too roughly or quickly. It can take up to seven or eight months to grow out of, so until that time it is very important that your babies are securely tucked in by their bed covers.
- If your babies are feeding at 5/6am, treat it as a night feed. It should be done as quickly as possible in a dimly lit room without any eye contact or talking. Change their nappies only if really necessary.
- Do not drop the 10pm feed until your babies have started on solids. If they go through a growth spurt before they start solids, they can be offered extra milk at this feed. This reduces the chances of them waking early due to hunger.

Your questions answered

Q How many hours' sleep a day does a newborn baby need?
A • Depending on weight and whether or not the baby was premature, most newborns need approximately 16 hours a day, broken up into a series of short and long sleeps. Small babies and premature babies tend to need more

sleep, possibly up to 18 hours a day. If your babies weigh under 2.7kg (6lb) at birth, you will probably find that they doze on and off between feeds. Once they weigh 2.7–3.2kg (6–7lb), you will probably find that they are capable of staying awake for an hour or so and sleeping for at least one longer spell of 3–4 hours during a 24-hour period. By the age of one month, most babies who are feeding well and gaining weight (180–240g/6–8oz a week) are capable of sleeping for one longer stretch of 4–5 hours between feeds.

Q My twin girls are now two weeks old and are constantly sleepy. I am trying hard to keep them awake as recommended during the day, but they seem to drift off the whole time. This is particularly difficult during the evening feed at 6pm. After I feed one of my twins her half-feed, she falls asleep while her sister is taking the first half of her feed. How do I keep them awake long enough to last the whole feed?

A • If your first baby tends to fall asleep while the second baby is feeding, try taking her legs out of her baby-grow and encouraging a kick-around. This could help keep her alert enough to feed well. If your babies persist in being very sleepy, don't worry. Simply continue reinforcing the message of dark = sleep, light = awake. Just keeping them in light rooms during awake times should be enough for them to make the connection later on. In the meantime, remember that tiny babies do need a great deal of sleep, so they will continue sleeping a lot until they are ready to be more alert during the day.

Q My daughters are just over three weeks old, and at the moment both sleep in separate Moses baskets in the same room. I am not sure if this is the best idea as, more often than not, one will either not settle to sleep straight away and disturb the other during the 20 minutes of wind-down crying, or one will wake early and invariably wake the other. I know that there is an element of comfort in keeping them

both together, but I wonder if perhaps it would be better if they were in different rooms.

A • I have encountered this problem with twins and found separating them for a short period is the best way to get both of them into good sleeping habits. Once both of them were better at settling, we moved them back into the same room during the day, but they spent the nights apart as this ensured they both got the best amount of sleep. During their waking hours they spent a lot of time close together by sharing an activity mat, and while still small enough, I would put them together in a playpen under a musical mobile. They did not seem to mind at all being separated for sleep.

Q My twin boys are 12 weeks old and we have been following CLB routines since week three. Until very recently we were putting the boys down to sleep at 11pm and would generally get one waking from each of them in the night. We reduced the feed to 60ml (2oz) of formula milk and have tried separating them so that at least one of them will go through the night, but without success. How can I get them both to sleep through the night?

A • Even if your boys are the same weight, it is not uncommon for one to be ready to sleep through before the other. Try to encourage Twin One first, if he seems more able to get through the night. If he won't accept water, try a cuddle for five minutes. It may be that habit rather than hunger is waking him. He needs to be given 10 minutes to settle himself before you go in. If possible, put the boys out of earshot of each other temporarily until both of them are able to settle back to sleep without too much fuss.

• You can resolve the night-feeding issue by encouraging Twin One to last until 6am and feeding him then. Settle him straight back to sleep until 7.30am (when you can offer him a small top-up). In the meantime, you can finish giving Twin Two his 7am feed. This way they will both be ready to feed again at 10/10.30am. It could possibly take a week or 10 days before Twin One will manage to last until 7am. It helps to work in stages.

- With Twin Two I would continue to offer him a diluted feed when he wakes, but keep working on the 'core night' principle and get him to 3 or 4am before feeding him. Give him another week, then try to encourage him on to 4.30am. Just getting him on by 30 minutes at a time will eventually mean that he will sleep through.

- Try keeping the twin who wakes more and needs feeding for longer (Twin Two) in with you so that he is less likely to disturb Twin One.

- It is understandable that you are longing for the broken nights to be over, especially when you have two babies to cope with, but getting them to sleep through can take time. Try taking turns with your husband at night. It might be a good idea if one of you has Twin One for two nights, then swaps over to care for Twin Two. That way you should both get a few nights of more sleep.

Q I have 17-week-old twins and use the routines with their adjusted date of 11 weeks. Their morning nap is too early and also taken twice. This makes the lunchtime nap at completely the wrong time. I cannot keep the babies awake in the morning past 8.30am. This means they sleep from 11.30am to 12.30pm.

A • As your twins get older, they will be able to stay awake for longer periods of time. It is not unusual for babies of their age to be ready to sleep for one to one-and-a-half hours after waking. This is especially true with your babies, who were born early. The routines state that a baby of this age can be awake for up to two hours before needing a nap, but many are ready long before this. Keep working at prolonging the time they can be awake. One good way is to top and tail them at 8.20am if they are getting tired. This should help them stay awake until 8.45am.

- While they are still tired at 8.30am, let them have a sleep until 9.10/9.15am. By feeding the twins earlier than 11am and offering them the second part of their feed before going down, it may be possible to get them to sleep for a longer stretch at lunchtime. Offer them half their feed at 10.30am rather than letting them fall asleep. If they are unable to stay awake, let them have a 15-minute catnap before 11.15am. Offer them the second part of their feed around 11.30/11.45am. Then encourage them to stay awake until 12/12.15pm. Hunger is often the cause of waking during this nap. By giving them a split feed, you may find this nap begins to lengthen.

- Until this happens, the twins will need to have a nap in the afternoon. Provided this does not become too long, or stretch beyond 5pm, they should be ready to settle at 7pm. If the lunchtime sleep becomes longer, you may find they need only a really short nap in the afternoon, but will be tired earlier in the evening. If this happens, make their bedtime earlier. Fitting the routines in with your babies' needs can mean some juggling and tweaking to allow for what has happened earlier in the day.

- A lot of mothers find it easier to cope in the evenings if they continue to split-feed at 5/6pm. Although this technique is used in the routines during the early weeks, many babies seem to benefit from having part of their feed at 5pm and the remainder after their bath. It usually means that bathtime is less stressful because the baby is not so hungry.

- At this age it is reasonable to expect a baby to play for about 15–20 minutes before needing some attention. Some babies find this easier than others. With twins this can be very apparent. Keep encouraging your babies to play alone by sitting separately with them for short periods and engaging their attention with a toy. Then move away, but remain within sight, and talk to them from time to time. Use an encouraging voice to help them know that although you are not right beside them or holding them, you are still aware of what they are doing. Don't have too many toys out at once: two for each baby is plenty. You can take these away and replace them with something different after 10–15 minutes or so to help them play for longer periods without needing your attention all the time.

Q My five-month-old twin girls were born two months prematurely. They are now doing well on the routines, but they continue to wake in the night around 3/4am. Their daily milk intake has always been less than it should be for their weight. For the last three weeks I have started to use the 'core night' method, giving them only water when they wake up. This seemed to work at the beginning, pushing their waking time to 4.30/5.30am for a couple of nights, but there is no pattern to it. Sometimes they sleep until 7am, but at other times they wake around 6am.

A • Getting your girls to sleep right through the night without waking and without the need for water may mean trying to increase their daily intake by using split feeds. Between three and four months there is often a growth spurt. The fact that your daughters were born prematurely is probably the reason they cannot sustain sleeping through for more than a few nights. To help them take a good feed at 10pm, continue to wake them at this time, but split the feed in two, adding an extra 30–60ml (1–2oz) to each bottle. To do this effectively, you may need to wake them around 9.45pm in order for them to be ready to take the first half of their feed at 10pm. Make sure they are fully awake before giving it to them. Once finished, allow them to have some quiet kicking time until 11.15pm. Although you need them to stay awake, don't overstimulate them, as you want them to settle down easily. At 11.15pm change them and give each of them the second half of their feed in their room with the lights dimmed. This lengthened period of being awake, combined with a slightly bigger feed, should help them to push on further in the night. Note that it is best to make this feed in two bottles for each baby so that the one offered at 11.15pm will be fresh and have no stale milk tainting the teat. If the girls begin to stir at 3/4am, leave them 5–10 minutes before going in, to see if they are able to settle themselves back to sleep. As they have shown, they are able to get through the night without milk, so see if you are able to settle them without giving water. You may need to hold them for five minutes to let them calm themselves into sleepiness again.

- If they are in sleeping bags, make sure they are well tucked in, with a sheet placed lengthways over them and well secured at each side. The Moro reflex can still be strong at this age, and when the girls enter a light sleep cycle, it may disturb them enough to wake fully. Until a baby is sleeping through the night from 11pm to 7am, and has consistently done so for two weeks, it is better to split the feed at 5/6pm. As your girls have a low daily milk intake, they could benefit from this. It also means that they do not take too big a feed at 6.30pm, which may in turn cause them to have a smaller feed at 10pm. Once they have slept through on a regular basis for two weeks, you can gradually reduce the amount given at 5pm, dropping it back to one feed at 6.30pm, when you feel they are able to get through the night without waking.

Common problems in the first few months | 5

'Wound up about winding' – Alice

Paul and I are quite similar in that we both want to do things the best way possible. Once we got over the competitive swaddling when the girls were very tiny, we moved on to winding.

There was a period at about two months when it seemed that no sooner were you celebrating the fact that both babies had taken a good feed and were in clean baby-grows ready for sleep, both little faces smiling up at you, than from out of those gorgeous little mouths would pour the complete collective 100ml. The feeling of desperation from being back at square one when all you want to do is crawl off to bed and sleep is the pits.

We didn't know why they were doing it. And I still don't know the dictionary definitions of reflux, possetting or just plain old vomit, but Paul and I like solutions, so we tried them all. Those poor little mites probably went through a phase of not knowing what pure milk tasted like any more. Before their bottles they had drops of Infacol, like little baby birds, and a good swig of gripe water mixed in with the milk. But we were convinced that the real secret of their ability to keep the milk down, enabling us to get back into bed as soon as possible, was directly related to the amount of time we winded them. We would clutch at any straw for a night's sleep.

Paul became fixated by winding. For him, anything less than 15 minutes of back-patting and rubbing was a potential disaster. I was much less fastidious and far more impatient to get downstairs and flop on the sofa. Paul was always there, conscientiously patting, long after I had disappeared to 'check on supper'. We were complete suckers for any new technique, and one particular night nanny, who came to let us sleep for the night, showed us her own particular, bizarre, circular stroking method. It involved huge circular movements all around the baby's back, then gentle circles around the stomach. We perfected those moves like a boy band with a new dance routine. We were lucky that my parents were patient with us as new parents. When they came to visit they were very good at not laughing while we talked them through the latest definitive way to wind a baby. Of course, the trouble with trying 50 things at once is that you are not sure which one is working . . . and long after the girls started keeping their milk down, they were still awash with Infacol and gripe water and being rubbed on the back for hours on end.

I have always considered the girls as individuals. It is impossible not to do so. Even during pregnancy they had different characters: Dora kicking and tumbling, while poor squashed Phoebe just hung around patiently, giving the occasional wiggle. But for some reason I expected them to sleep and feed at identical times. I found it a problem to adapt to their different needs and habits. I felt that I needed to treat them the same, but it was difficult when Phoebe took twice as long to drink as Dora. I couldn't wind Dora while feeding Phoebe – I just needed them to be doing the same thing at the same time. This was probably one of the reasons I put off doing the *CLB* routines for a few weeks. I think I was concerned that I would be exaggerating my desire for an effective, efficient routine and not catering for them as very different little people. The routines looked quite complicated and seemed to account for every second of the day, whereas I needed space in my day to accommodate their individuality. I needn't have worried; I should just have got on with it. As soon as the girls started feeding and sleeping at regular times, it all made sense. I could anticipate when they would be hungry or sleepy, and that gave me time to make sure they were both satisfied.

Looking back, I know there were a few weeks when Paul and I both thought we had been given two of those awful 'non-stop crying' babies. Before we got into any kind of routine, there were long, long hours in the early evening when they were just inconsolable. It is hard enough to cope with the sound of one baby crying, but two of them crying for two hours is frankly more than a lactating mother can bear. We were both so exhausted that we found ourselves snapping instructions at each other. 'Put her on your shoulder, for goodness sake.' 'Stop jiggling her, she'll be sick.' 'Jiggle her, she needs movement.' They were awful, desperate hours. Those little kitten-in-distress cries shot directly to our nervous systems, but we remained a team and we worked it out. Paul had a special jiggle and rock technique and I had a smattering of tunes from West End musicals, which seemed to calm them or bore them into sleep. I found a tune from *My Fair Lady*, with my own invented lyrics, was particularly effective.

Once we did start to follow the routines seriously, we found it much easier to anticipate the babies' needs, and we realised that there is more to caring for a baby than feeding, burping and cuddling. If ever one or other baby got fractious, I would immediately turn to the 'Common Problems' chapter and do a checklist of all the reasons why she might be unsettled. It is amazing how, after reading that chapter several times, the list becomes ingrained in your subconscious and how quickly you can get to the root of the problem.

Once we got the hang of pre-empting the girls' needs and immediately responding to them in the right way, life became so much happier for all of us. Two happy babies means two happy parents. My heart really goes out to parents when I see them struggling for hours on end with a screaming baby and just accepting that it is normal because 'that is what babies do'. Believe you me, I know from experience that it is not normal for young babies to be fretful and spend hours crying. If you are following the *CLB* sleeping and feeding guidelines and you find your baby is still getting upset, please look for other reasons. As Gina constantly says, young babies do cry for reasons other than hunger and tiredness.

~

Pinpointing the problem

When your babies are very tiny and they become fretful and unsettled it is, of course, wise to assume that the problem is hunger and offer them a feed – even if it is before the time I recommend in the routines for their age. One of the main reasons I've found for very young breast-fed babies being unsettled in the evening is usually hunger. If you find that your babies feed well, stay awake for a short spell after feeds, then sleep well until the next feed, but are unsettled in the evening, it is very possible that the cause is hunger. In this case, I strongly recommend that for a few nights you try topping them up with a small amount of expressed milk after their bath. If they then settle well, you will know that your milk is low at that time of the evening and you will have to decide how best to deal with this problem (see page 54 for ideas).

However, if you find that your babies are unsettled in the evening or, indeed, at any other times of the day, despite being well fed, it is important to eliminate other possible reasons for their fretfulness. All too often I hear people saying that it is normal for babies to cry a lot in the early days 'as that's what babies do'. During my many years of caring for young babies, I have indeed encountered some who were fretful in the early days no matter what I did to calm them. But I have to stress that such babies were just a few among the hundreds I cared for. Whenever I had a very unsettled baby I would go through every possibility before accepting that there was nothing that could be done to improve things. Babies have many needs other than food, sleep and physical contact. The pages that follow describe some of the main causes of fretfulness or excessive crying in the early days.

Burping

It is important to follow your babies' respective leads regarding when to stop and wind them. Twins are bound to be different from each other, so don't be surprised by this. If you constantly interrupt a feed to get wind up, the baby can become upset and frustrated, which will cause more wind than the feed itself. As Alice says, you can easily become obsessed with winding. Very few babies need to be burped more than once during a feed and once at the end.

A breast-feeding baby will pull himself off the breast when he is ready to burp. If you are feeding both babies together, this can cause problems if one baby pulls off and wants to wind, while the other one wants to continue feeding. If you find this happening to you because one of your babies is particularly windy, it would be worth feeding them separately for a short while to see if this improves the problem.

Bottle-fed babies will normally drink half to three-quarters of their feed and pull themselves off to be burped. If you adopt the correct holding position, each baby should bring his wind up quickly and easily both during and at the end of the feed. If your baby does not bring up the wind within a few minutes, it is best to leave it and try later. More often than not he will bring it up after he has been laid flat for his nappy change.

Occasionally, a baby passing excessive wind from his rear end can suffer considerable discomfort and become very distressed. If breast-feeding, keep a close eye on your diet to see if a particular food or drink is causing the wind. Citrus fruits or drinks taken in excess can cause severe wind in some babies. The other culprits are chocolate and excessive dairy intake.

Special care should be taken to ensure that the babies are each reaching the hind milk. Too much fore milk can cause explosive bowel movements and excessive passing of wind.

With a bottle-fed baby who is already feeding from the special anti-colic bottles, the cause of the excessive wind is usually overfeeding. If your baby is regularly drinking 90–180ml (3–6oz) a day more than the amount advised on the packet, and constantly putting on in excess of 240g (8oz) of weight each week, cut back on a couple of his feeds (either the 2.30pm or 5pm) for a few days to see if there is any improvement. A 'sucky' baby could be offered a dummy after the smaller feeds to satisfy his sucking needs.

Sometimes a teat with a hole either too small or too large for your baby's needs can cause excessive wind. Experiment with the different sizes of teats; using a smaller hole at a couple of the feeds can sometimes help a baby who is drinking some of his feeds too quickly.

Colic

Colic is a common problem for babies under three months. It can make life miserable for the baby and the parents, and to date there is no cure for it. There are over-the-counter medications, but most parents with a baby suffering from severe colic say that they are of little help. Although a baby can suffer from colic at any time of the day, the most common time seems to be between 6pm and midnight. Parents resort to endless feeding, rocking and patting, even driving the baby around the block, but most of these seem to bring little or no relief. I have spoken to thousands of parents over the years and in the majority of cases the excessive crying that is often called colic is usually caused by two main things: hunger and overtiredness. In some cases it arises from a combination of both. If one or both of your babies are crying and unsettled in the evening, I urge you to try topping up with some expressed milk and bringing the bedtime forward slightly to ensure that they are not getting overtired. If this does not work, I suggest you try following the advice in the box opposite.

Colic usually disappears by four months of age, but by that time the baby has usually learnt all the wrong sleep associations, so the parents are no further forward. The method described below, along with the routines, will encourage a baby who has suffered from colic and developed the wrong sleep associations to sleep through the night, normally within a couple of weeks.

Tips for dealing with colic

- Check whether the colic is being caused by demand-feeding rather than the mother's diet (see Burping, page 93).
- Depending on the age and symptoms of the colicky baby, and how often he is feeding through-out the evening and in the middle of the night, you could introduce sugar water. With a baby aged between one and three months who is feeding excessively in the night and consistently putting on more than the recommended weight gain each week, replace one of the night feeds with some sugar water. When the baby wakes in the night give 120ml (4oz) of cool boiled water mixed with half a teaspoon of sugar to settle him. Plain boiled water does not appear to have the same effect. The following day wake the baby at 7am, regardless of how little sleep he has had in the night, and proceed with the routine throughout the day to 6.30pm. Always offer a breast-fed baby a top-up of expressed milk to ensure that he has had enough to drink. This avoids him needing to feed again in two hours, which is a common pattern among babies suffering from colic. With a bottle-fed baby, always make sure that the 2.30pm feed is smaller than the 6.30pm feed so that he feeds well at the latter.
- With an older baby of three months or more, try to reduce middle-of-the-night feeds to only one. It is important to ensure that the baby feeds well at 6.15pm, offering a top-up of expressed milk at

this time if necessary. A low milk supply in the early evening is often the cause of a baby feeding little and often, which can lead to him not digesting feeds properly.

- With babies who have developed the wrong sleep associations as a result of colic, you may have to consider some form of sleep training. This is always a last resort and should be used only if all other methods have failed. However, if it is approached properly, the problem can usually be resolved within 3–4 nights. Then, when they are going down happily and sleeping well until the 10.30pm feed, things will also improve in the middle of the night. As they will have slept well and gone a full four hours since their last feed, they will feed well and go on to last for an even longer spell in the night. Depending on their age, they are given either a feed or sugar water. A baby of three months or older who is capable of going from the last feed through to 6/7am should be given sugar water for a week. When the pattern of once-a-night waking is established, gradually reduce the amount of sugar until he is taking plain water.

Crying

Many of the twins I have cared for were crying from one feed to the next before I was called in to help sort the problem out. The sad reality is that if the parents of those twins had started to establish a routine, weeks and often months of constant crying could have been avoided. One of the reasons that the *CLB* routines have become so popular is that they structure feeding and sleeping from the very beginning, which has the effect of making crying virtually non-existent. The *CLB* philosophy is that no baby should have to cry to have his needs met. Of course, babies *do* cry, but excessive crying, where the baby is calm only if being rocked or held, is, in my opinion, not normal.

Obviously, all new parents are anxious to make their newborn babies' introduction to the world a happy one. As we all associate crying with pain or unhappiness, it is understandable that new parents will be prepared to do virtually anything to stop their babies crying. A newborn baby's only way of communicating is by crying, but do not fall into the trap of thinking that the only way of dealing with it is by feeding: there are several other possible reasons.

Note that very young babies go through a more unsettled stage around 3–6 weeks, which tends to coincide with a growth spurt. At such times a common worry among parents of crying babies is that putting them down to sleep and allowing them to settle themselves could be psychologically damaging. Provided your babies have been well fed and that you have followed the routines regarding awake periods and wind-down time, your babies will not suffer psychological damage if they are allowed to fuss for 5–10 minutes to get off to sleep. In the long term you will have happy, contented babies who have learnt to settle themselves to sleep. Research shows that many babies who have learnt the wrong sleep associations and who go on to have long-term sleep problems often become much more disruptive during their school years.

The following text outlines the main reasons a healthy baby cries. Check each one to eliminate the possible causes of your babies' crying so that you can satisfy their real needs.

Boredom

Even a newborn baby needs to be awake some of the time. When I looked after twins I used to have books, music and two types of toys: noisy ones for wakeful periods, and calm ones for winding-down time. Encourage each baby to be awake for a short spell after the day feeds. Babies under one month love to look at anything black and white, especially pictures of faces, and the ones that fascinate them most are the faces of Mummy and Daddy. With twins it is hard to give each of them individual attention. If one baby is happy amusing himself but the other one is demanding more attention, do not feel guilty that you seem to be ignoring the happy child in favour of the other. In my experience, the attention you give each one usually balances out over time, and you should not beat yourself up trying to make them equal all the time.

Hunger

This is most likely to happen in the evening, and may occur even if your babies are making a good weight gain each week and you feel you are producing enough milk. Many mothers I know can produce a lot of milk during the early part of the day, but come the evening, when tiredness creeps in, their milk supply can really decrease. This is particularly true for mothers of twins. If your babies are very unsettled in the evening, I suggest you try offering them a top-up of expressed milk after the bath. If you express a little before each of your morning feeds, you should manage to get just enough to top them up. If they then settle well, hunger is the cause of their previous distress and you will have to try resting more in the afternoon to help increase your milk for the evening feeds.

Tiredness

Babies under six weeks tend to get tired after one hour of being awake. Although they may not be quite ready to sleep, they need to be kept quiet and calm. I advise that you take them either to their room so that they can wind down gradually, or keep them in a calm and quiet part of the house. Try not to allow visitors to overstimulate them if they are still awake after one hour.

Wind

All babies take in a certain amount of wind while feeding – bottle-fed babies more so than breast-fed ones. Given the opportunity, most babies bring up their wind easily. If you suspect that your babies' crying is caused by wind, check that you are allowing enough time between feeds. A breast-fed baby needs at least three hours to digest a full feed, and a formula-fed baby should be allowed three-and-a-half to four hours. This timing is made from the beginning of one feed to the beginning of the next.

Excessive weight gain from overfeeding can also be the cause of wind in the early days. My experience with twins is that they normally gain 240–300g (8–10oz) a week early on. But if they continue to put on this amount of weight consistently over a period of several weeks and are suffering from wind pains, overfeeding could possibly be the cause. This is particularly likely if they weigh nearly 3.6kg (8lb) and are still feeding two or three times a night. If you do have any concerns about whether you might be overfeeding your baby you should discuss them with your health visitor.

Dummies

Alice dislikes the sight of dummies, and I know many parents are of a similar view. Speaking personally, I do not have a problem with young babies having a dummy, and I certainly think they helped me cope with many sets of twins. Some babies are more sucky than others, and if you find that one or both of yours is calmer if allowed to suck on a dummy, ignore the critics and allow him the comfort that sucking provides. This is particularly true if your baby is suffering from wind pains due to overfeeding.

Those who tell you that babies should be allowed to find their thumb obviously do not realise that very young babies lack the coordination that this requires. While the majority are able to find their thumb, few can keep it in their mouth long enough to achieve any sucking pleasure. It takes nearly three months for a baby to develop enough coordination to keep his thumb in his mouth for any length of time.

If used with discretion, a dummy can be a great asset, especially for a sucky baby. Never allow either of your babies to have a dummy in the cot or allow them to suck themselves to sleep on a dummy. Use it to calm them and, if necessary, settle them at sleep times, **but remove it before they fall asleep**. Allowing a baby to fall asleep with a dummy in his mouth is one of the worst sleep association problems to solve. He can end up waking several times a night, and each time he will expect the dummy to get back to sleep. This problem can easily be avoided if the dummy is removed just before he drops off to sleep.

If used selectively, dummies are rejected by most babies by the age of three months. If a baby reaches four months and is still using a dummy, gradually wean him from using it over a period of two weeks by reducing the number of times you allow him to use it each day; any longer could lead to real attachment problems.

There are two types of dummy available: one has a round, cherry-type teat, while the other, called an orthodontic teat, has a flat shape. Some experts claim that the orthodontic teat shape is better for the baby's mouth, but the problem with this type is that most young babies cannot hold it in for very long. Choose the cherry-type teat to avoid an open bite – often the result of a dummy being used excessively once the teeth have come through.

Whichever type of dummy you choose, buy several, thus allowing them to be changed frequently. The utmost attention should be paid to cleanliness when using a dummy; it should be washed and sterilised after each use.

Hiccups

Tiny babies often get hiccups after a feed, and very few get distressed by them. If they occur after a night-time feed and a baby is due for a sleep, it is advisable to put him down regardless. If you wait until the hiccups are finished, there is a greater chance of his falling asleep in your arms, which is something to be avoided. If either of your babies is among the few who get upset by hiccups, give him the recommended dose of gripe water.

Possetting

It is very common for some babies to bring up a small amount of milk after a feed or while being burped. This is called 'possetting', and for most babies it does not create a problem.

If one or both of your babies is regularly gaining more than 240g (8oz) of weight each week, it could be that he is drinking too much. With a bottle-fed baby, the problem is easily solved, as you are able to see how much he is drinking and therefore slightly reduce the amount at the feeds when he appears to posset more. It is more difficult to tell how much a breast-fed baby is drinking, but by keeping a note of which feeds cause most possetting, and reducing the time on the breast at those feeds, the possetting may be reduced.

If one or both of your babies is possetting excessively and not gaining weight, it could be that he is suffering from a condition called 'reflux' (see below). In this case, your doctor can prescribe a medication to be given either before or with a feed, which helps to keep the milk down. With babies who are inclined to bring up milk, it is important to keep them as upright as possible after a feed, and special care should be taken when burping.

Any baby bringing up an entire feed twice in a row could be at risk of dehydration or other medical conditions and should be seen by a doctor immediately.

Reflux

Sometimes a baby displaying all the symptoms of colic actually has a condition called gastro-oesophageal reflux. The muscle at the lower end of the oesophagus is too weak to keep the milk in the baby's stomach, so it comes back up, along with acid from the stomach, causing a very painful burning sensation in the oesophagus. Excessive possetting is one of the symptoms of reflux. However, not all babies with reflux actually sick up the milk, and these babies may be misdiagnosed as having colic. They are often very difficult to feed, constantly arching their backs and screaming. They also tend to get very irritable when laid flat, and no amount of cuddling or rocking will calm them when they are like this. If your baby displays these symptoms, insist that your doctor does a reflux test.

It is important that a baby with reflux is not overfed and is kept as upright as possible during and after feeding. Some babies may need medication for several months until the muscles tighten up. Fortunately, the majority of babies outgrow the condition by the time they reach one year old. If you think that your baby is suffering from reflux, it is essential that you do not allow anyone to dismiss the pains as colic. Reflux is very stressful for both baby and parents, and it essential to seek help from a GP or health visitor who has experience of babies with colic. Do not be frightened of asking for a second opinion from a paediatrician. If reflux is not the problem, you will have at least eliminated it as a possible cause. If it is the problem, some medication will save your baby months of misery from the pain that it causes.

Sleepy feeder

Sometimes a very sleepy baby may be inclined to keep dozing during a feed, but if he does not want to take the required amount, he will end up wanting to feed again in an hour or two. This is very true of twins, and during the first few weeks your babies will probably take what seems to be for ever to feed. But once they reach nearer one month or around 3.2kg (7lb) in weight, this sleepiness does start to get less. It is worth putting a bit of extra effort into these early feeds to ensure that sleepy feeding does not lead to a problem of feeding little and often for weeks down the line. Making a little effort in the early days to keep your baby awake enough to drink the correct amount at each feed, and at the times given on the routine, will be worth it in the long term.

Some babies prefer to take half the feed, have a nappy change or kick around for 10–15 minutes, then take the rest. The important thing is not to force them to stay awake by talking a lot or jiggling them about too much. If you put them under their playgym or cot mobile for 10 minutes, you will probably find that they get enough of a second wind to take a bit more of the feed. During the first months, allow up to 45 minutes for a feed. Obviously, if either or both of them do not feed well at a particular feed, and wake early from their sleep, they must be fed. Do not try to stretch them to the next feed, or they will be so tired that the next feed will then become another sleepy feed. Top them up and treat the feed like a night feed, then try to settle them back to sleep so that you can get the feeding back on track by the evening.

Establishing a routine | 6

'Relief at last' – Alice

Once we started the routines seriously, it was a relief. I carried 'that book', as it became known, from room to room, religiously following quantities and timings. I must admit I didn't follow Gina's reminders to have something to eat and drink, as I had usually had three pieces of toast already and really didn't need encouraging to have more.

I found it such a relief to be depending on someone else who knew what she was talking about. Very importantly at this stage, when we were both exhausted and crabby, the book also took the blame and responsibility away from us. Paul and I became much more of a team, learning a new set of rules together and searching for answers in the well-thumbed pages when things seemed to go wrong.

Within days of starting the routines, and much to the relief of our neighbours, the girls stopped their manic crying in the early evening. It became obvious that the routines were what they needed. Their tiny bodies had been literally crying out for some kind of order. Now they were getting more food and less sleep during the day, they were full and tired as they hit their cots at night.

I remember looking at the routines as I lay in bed 'gestating' before the babies arrived, and thinking how complicated they seemed – even a little daunting to a first-time mother who can't yet imagine the reality of her babies. Looking back now, I realise it was the equivalent of a flight manual: the moment we were seated in the cockpit it was just what we needed – step-by-step instructions to creating well-fed, well-rested, contented babies. We had been doing okay tweaking all the right knobs and buttons for take-off, but there was simply a much better way of getting airborne.

The week that the girls started sleeping through the night was such a fantastic breakthrough. It was the last week in August, so they were about to be three months old. We were due to go on holiday to France soon afterwards, and had decided that to get some sleep we would ask a friend's au pair to come with us and just do the nights between 7pm and 7am. She kindly agreed and our shifts were carefully calculated and passports packed when the girls decided that they would sleep without a squeak from 7pm to 7am. It was amazing. We had not done anything outstandingly different – just regulated their food and sleep patterns.

I know that during the girls' first two months at home we were incredibly jumpy – perhaps all new parents are. When one of them cried we would leap up and start going through the checklist of what could be wrong, nervously trying to quell their anxiety and ours. When we had a structure to the day, we became much calmer because we could anticipate what was wrong when a baby cried. We weren't so stressed around them after they had a routine, and I am positive they picked up on the calmness their parents were now able to show.

We both became much more confident around the babies, and really began to enjoy the different parts of our routine. 'Nappy off and kicking time' at the beginning and end of the day was an especially happy time, with lots of tickling, cuddling and unscheduled peeing on the bed (them not me).

I do not know how a single parent begins to cope with multiple babies; I suppose you just get on with it. I have been so lucky to have a partner who has thrown himself into parenthood 100 per cent. One evening when we had first started following CLB routines, I was doing the sterilising when Paul came running anxiously downstairs waving the book in one hand. 'What are we going to do? The builders haven't put a dimmer in the babies' room and Gina says we have to dim the lights.'

I think my parents came to dread the words 'Gina says' because they heard them so often. But when they saw their happy granddaughters they completely embraced what we were doing and followed our lead. I have always been one for charts and lists, so virtually every one of the babies' breaths, feeds and poos was recorded and stuck on the fridge door. It was such a relief knowing that if my parents came to help, they could just take over the routine where I'd left it. Everyone wrote down how much milk they had taken, and totals were totted up like *Countdown* calculations at the end of each day. If we had hit the Gina jackpot number required, we were all okay – they would sleep and so would we.

There is obviously a memory hormone that hits parents at the time of birth and fades as the child grows. By the age of 60, memories of parenting are somewhat shot. If only the old wives' advice were true: 'I left my babies in the pram in the garden for three hours every day and never heard a squeak' or 'No child of mine ever cried between being put to bed and us waking them up'. I often thanked my lucky stars that we had twins and so avoided much of the well-intended but infuriating advice.

In summary, it was all very simple stuff. As the girls had a routine, we had a routine. Somehow the structure gave us something solid to cling on to during those early days and nights. I had hit a low a couple of months after they were born, and having had a career with a lot of lovely attention and brain power, I was finding it hard to get myself out of my jeans and calculate anything more arduous than the milk totals for the day. I had worked a little in the very early days because I was too confused to say no, but the time came when I occasionally needed to be able to walk out of the front door empty-handed for my own sanity. Thanks to *CLB* routines I could plan my forays into the world to suit my babies, knowing that they were safe in the hands of their grandparents or their father, and that I would return home to the routine and not spend days undoing whatever the eager helpers might have done in my absence.

~

Understanding *CLB* routines for feeding

The important thing to understand about establishing the *CLB* routines is that they are not like the old-fashioned four-hourly routines that forced babies to feed and sleep at certain times regardless of their individual needs. The times of the feedings given in this book are intended as guidelines. If one or both of your babies is not managing to get to the times on the routine for his or her age, do not worry; just stick to the routine that they are happy in and watch for the signs when they are ready to go longer between feeds. In order to get your babies into a good feeding and sleeping routine, you must ensure that when they are ready to increase milk feeds, you structure the feeding and sleeping so that they increase their daytime feeds rather than their night-time ones. This is the key to getting your babies to sleep for longer as soon as they are physically capable of doing so. The following guidelines explain what you are aiming for long term to ensure that this happens.

The 6–7am feed

Depending on what time they have each fed in the night, your babies will probably wake up between 6am and 7am, but the first to feed should always be woken at 6.45am regardless. Remember that one of the main keys to getting your babies to sleep through the night is to ensure that once they are physically capable of taking bigger feeds, they take their daily requirements between 7am and 11pm.

If one or both babies have had a full feed between 5am and 6am, they will need a top-up by 7.30am to keep the feeding and sleeping times on track. Regardless of whether they are breast-fed or bottle-fed, the only way to keep babies in a good routine is to begin the day at 6.45am. Once they are sleeping through the night, they should be at their hungriest at this feed.

During growth spurts, breast-fed babies should be given longer on the breast or extra feeds to ensure that their increased needs are met. If you have been expressing, you can reduce this by 30ml (1oz) to ensure that their needs are immediately met. If you have not expressed, you can still follow the feeding times from the routine for their age, but you will have to top them up with a short breast-feed before their naps. If you do this for a week or so, this should help increase your milk supply. A sign that this has happened is that your babies will sleep well at the naps and not be so interested at the next feed. Once this happens, you can gradually decrease the length of time that you top up for, until you are back on your original feeding schedule. Formula-fed babies should have their feeds increased by 30ml (1oz) when they are regularly draining their bottle.

By seven months

If your babies are eating a full breakfast of cereal, fruit and perhaps small pieces of toast, you should aim to cut back the amount offered to them from the bottle. Try to divide the feed between a drink and giving the remainder with the cereal. Always encourage them to take at least 150–180ml (5–6oz) before they are given their solids.

If you are still breast-feeding, gradually reduce the time they are on the breast, then give them their solids and, finally, a further short feed from the breast. Keep a very close eye that you do not allow them to increase their solids so much that they cut back too much on their breast-feed.

Each baby still needs a minimum of 500–600ml (17–20oz) a day inclusive of milk used in cooking or on cereal, divided between 3–4 milk feeds.

By ten months

If your babies are formula-fed, encourage them both to take all their milk from a beaker. Ensure that you still offer milk at the start of the meal. Once they have taken 150–180ml (5–6oz) of their milk, offer them some cereal, then offer them the remainder of their milk.

It is important that they each have at least 180–240ml (6–8oz) of milk divided between the beaker and the breakfast cereal.

If you are still breast-feeding, offer each in turn the first breast, then the solids, then the breast again.

Your babies each need a minimum of 500–600ml (17–20oz) a day inclusive of milk used in cooking or on cereal, divided between 2–3 milk feeds.

The 10–11am feed

During the first few weeks, the majority of babies who have fed between 6am and 7am will wake looking for a feed around 10am. Even if your babies do not wake looking for a feed, it is important that you wake them both in turn. Remember that the aim is to ensure that your babies feed regularly during the day so that they need to wake only once for a feed between 11pm and 6/7am.

In the early days many babies would happily sleep 4–5 hours between feeds during the day. Regardless of whether they are breast-fed or bottle-fed, within a very short period of time this usually leads to several night-time feeds as the babies attempt to make up for their daily nutritional needs.

Too few feeds during the day in the early weeks also does little to help establish a good milk supply for a breast-feeding mother, and the babies feeding several times at night soon exhausts the mother so much that her milk supply is reduced even further.

Around six weeks they may show signs of being happy to go longer from the 7am feed, and the 10am feed can gradually be pushed to 10.30am. However, a baby who is feeding at 5/6am and being topped up at 7.30am would probably still need to feed at 10am, as would the baby who has too small a feed at 7am.

Once they are each sleeping through the night, or taking only a small feed in the night, they should have the biggest feed of the day at 6.45/7am. If they feed well, they should be happy to last until 11am before needing another feed. However, if you feed them before they really need it, they may not feed well and, as a result, may sleep poorly at the lunchtime nap. This will have a knock-on effect so that each subsequent feed and nap has to be given earlier, and may result in the baby waking up at 6am or earlier the following morning. This feed would be the next one to be increased during growth spurts.

By six to seven months

When your babies are eating breakfast you can start to make this feed later, eventually settling somewhere between 11am and 11.45am. This will be the pattern for three meals a day at the end of six months, at which stage the milk feed will be replaced with a drink of well-diluted juice or water from a beaker.

It is important that you introduce the tier system of feeding, which involves alternating between milk and solids during a feed, so that the babies gradually cut back on the milk feed and increase their solids.

By seven months

When your babies are on a proper balanced diet of solids, which includes solid protein with lunch, it is important that this feed should be replaced with a drink of water or well-diluted juice. Formula milk given with a protein meal can reduce iron absorption by up to 50 per cent. Give most of the solids before the drink so that they don't fill up with liquid first.

The 2–2.30pm feed

During the first few months, make this feed smaller so that your babies feed really well at the 5/6.15pm feed. If for some reason the babies feed badly at the 2.30pm feed, or fed earlier, increase this feed accordingly so that they maintain their daily milk quota.

If one or both babies are very hungry and regularly drain the bottle at this feed, you can give the full amount provided they do not take less at the next feed. For breast-fed babies allow longer on the breast if they are not happily managing to get through to the next feed.

By eight months

When your babies are having three full solid meals a day and their lunchtime milk feed has been replaced with water or well-diluted juice, you will probably need to increase this feed so that they are getting their respective daily milk quota in three milk feeds. However, if they cut back on the last milk feed of the day, it would be advisable to keep this milk feed smaller and make up the daily quota by using milk in cereals and cooking. Each baby still needs a minimum of 500–600ml (18–20oz) a day, inclusive of milk used on breakfast cereal and in cooking.

By nine to twelve months

Bottle-fed babies should be given their milk from a beaker at this stage, which should automatically result in a decrease in the amount they drink. If this is not the case and either baby starts to lose interest in his morning or evening feed, you could cut right back on this feed. If they are each getting 540ml (18oz) of milk a day (inclusive of milk used in cooking and on cereal), plus a full balanced diet of solids, you could cut this feed altogether. By one year of age each baby needs a minimum of 350ml (12oz) a day, inclusive of milk used in cooking and on cereal.

The 5–7pm feed

It is important that both babies always have a good feed at this time if you want them to settle well between 7pm and 10/11pm. They should not be fed milk after 3.15pm as it could put them off taking a really good feed at this time.

In the first few weeks this feed is split between 5pm and 6.15pm so that the babies are not getting too frantic during their bath. Once your babies have slept through the night for two weeks, the 5pm feed can be dropped. I do not recommend dropping the split feed until this happens as a larger feed at

6.15pm could result in your babies taking even less at the last feed, resulting in an earlier waking time. With many of the twins that I cared for, I kept giving them a split feed until solids were introduced to ensure that they were getting enough milk during the day. Once you eliminate the 5pm feed and the babies are taking a full feed after their bath, they might cut down dramatically on their last feed of the day, which could result in an early waking. Breast-fed babies not settling at 7pm should be offered a top-up of expressed milk.

By four to five months

If either of your babies has started solids early, he should be given most of his milk before the solids as milk is still the most important form of nutrition at this age. Most babies would be taking at least 210–240ml (7–8oz) of formula at this age.

If they are weaned and very tired at this feed, and you are struggling to get them to take all their milk plus any solids you have been advised to introduce, adjust the feeding times. Try giving two-thirds of each milk feed at around 5.30pm, followed by the solids, then delay their bath to around 6.25pm. After the bath they can then be offered the remainder of their milk feed. If formula-feeding, it is advisable to make up two separate bottles to ensure that the milk is fresh.

Breast-fed babies who reach five months, are weaned and are now starting to wake up before 10pm may not be getting enough at this time. Try giving a full breast-feed at 5.30pm, followed by the solids, with a bath at 6.15pm, followed by a top-up of expressed milk or formula after the bath. Babies who are not weaned would more than likely need to continue to have a split milk feed at 5/6.15pm until solids are introduced.

By six to seven months

Most babies will now be having tea at 5pm, followed by a full breast-feed or a 210–240ml (7–8oz) bottle. Once solids are established and the 10pm feed is dropped, you may find that if you are breast-feeding, your babies start to wake earlier. If this happens, I suggest you offer a top-up of expressed milk to ensure that they settle well at 7pm and sleep through until the morning.

By ten to twelve months

Bottle-fed babies should be taking all their milk from a beaker at one year. Babies who continue to feed from a bottle after this age are more prone to feeding problems as they continue to take large amounts, which take the edge off their appetite for solids.

Start encouraging your babies to take some of their milk from a beaker at 10 months so that by one year they are happy to take all their last feed from a beaker.

The 10–11pm feed

I recommend that all parents of breast-fed babies introduce bottles of either expressed milk or formula at this feed no later than the second week. This will help you to share the feeding responsibilities with a partner or other carer. It also helps to avoid the common problem of babies refusing to take a bottle at a later stage.

Totally breast-fed babies under three months who continue to wake up between 2am and 3am and show no sign of going a longer spell in the night may not be getting enough to eat at this time, as the breast milk supply is often at its lowest at this time of day.

If you choose to top up with expressed milk or formula rather than completely replacing the feed with a full bottle-feed, you must ensure that your babies have completely emptied the breast before they are offered the top-up feed.

It is easier to tell whether formula-fed babies are getting enough to eat at this feed. If you always increase the day feeds during your babies' growth spurts, they will probably never require more than 180ml (6oz) at this feed. However, some babies who weighed more than 4.5kg (10lb) at birth may reach a stage where they need more than this until they are well established on solids.

By three to four months

If your babies are totally breast-fed and are still waking up in the night despite being topped up with expressed milk at the late feed, it may be worth replacing the late breast-feeds with formula-feeds. Most formula-fed babies will be taking 210–240ml (7–8oz) per feed four times a day, and will want only a small feed of 120–180ml (4–6oz) at this time of night.

If formula-fed babies are not sleeping through the night at this age, it may be because they need a little extra at this feed, and even if it means they cut back on their morning feed, it may be worth offering them each an extra ounce or two.

Some babies simply refuse this feed at 3–4 months. If your babies are both feeding well from the breast four times a day, or taking a minimum of 1050ml (35oz) of formula a day, you can simply drop this feed, provided their weekly weight gain is still between 120–180g (4–6oz) each a week. However, if you find that they start to wake earlier again and will not settle back to sleep within 10 minutes or so, you will have to assume that they are hungry and feed them. You may then have to consider introducing the 10pm feed again until they are weaned and established on solids.

By four to six months

The majority of babies should be capable of sleeping through the night from their last feed at this age, provided they are taking their daily intake of milk between 7am and 11pm. Fully breast-fed babies may only manage to get through to around 5am until they are weaned.

Once your babies have been weaned and are established on three solid meals a day, this last feed should gradually reduce automatically. This will depend on how much solid food your babies are taking between six and seven months. If you have been advised to wean them earlier than six months, you should find that you can drop this feed fairly quickly once they reach six months. Babies who did not start solids until the recommended age of six months may still need a feed until they reach seven months. By this time, provided they are taking enough milk and solids during the day, you should be able to gradually reduce the amount they take and then eliminate it altogether.

The 2–3am feed

Newborn babies need to feed little and often during the first week, so when they wake it is best to assume that they are hungry and feed them. Newborn babies should never be allowed to go longer than three hours between feeds during the day and four hours between feeds in the night. This time runs from the beginning of one feed to the beginning of the next; it's not three hours from the end of one to the beginning of another.

Once your babies have regained their birth weight, they should start to settle into the 2–4 week routine. Provided they feed well between 10pm and 11pm, they should manage to get nearer to 2am.

By four to six weeks

Most babies weighing over 3.2kg (7lb) at birth and gaining a regular 180–240g (6–8oz) each week are capable of lasting a longer stretch between feeds during the night as long as:

- The baby is definitely over 4kg (9lb) in weight and taking his daily allowance of milk in the five feeds between 7am and 11pm.
- The baby is not sleeping more than four-and-a-half hours between 6.45am and 7pm.

By six to eight weeks

If one or both of your babies is over 4kg (9lb) in weight and gaining 180–240g (6–8oz) each week, but still waking between 2am and 3am, despite taking a good feed between 10pm and 11pm, try to settle them with some cool, boiled water. If they refuse to settle, you will have to feed them, but check page 149 for possible reasons why they are not going longer in the night.

If the babies do settle, they will probably wake up again around 5am, at which time you can give them each a full feed, followed by a top-up at 7/7.30am. This will help keep them on track with their feeding and sleeping pattern for the rest of the day.

Within a week, babies usually sleep until nearly 5am, gradually increasing their sleep time until 7am. During this stage, when one or both of the babies is taking a top-up at 7/7.30am instead of a full feed, they may not manage to get through to 10.45/11am for their next feed. You may need to give them half a feed at 10am, followed by the remainder plus a top-up just before they go down for their lunchtime nap, to ensure that they do not wake up early.

By three to four months

Both breast-fed and bottle-fed babies should be able to go for one long spell during the night by this age, provided they are getting their daily intake of milk between 6/7am and 10/11pm. The babies should be sleeping no more than three hours between 6.45am and 7pm.

If either baby insists on waking before 4/5am, refuses cool boiled water and will not settle without feeding, it would be advisable to keep a very detailed diary listing exact times and amounts of feeding and times of daytime naps. A baby who cuts right back on his 7am feed is probably waking out of habit rather than hunger.

Some breast-fed babies may still genuinely need to feed in the night if they are not getting enough at their last feed. If you are not already doing so, it is worth considering a top-up feed of expressed milk or formula, or a replacement formula-feed at the 10/11pm feed.

Whether you are breast-feeding or bottle-feeding, and provided your babies' weight gain is good, if you are convinced they are waking up from habit and refuse cool boiled water, try leaving it for 15–20 minutes before going to them. Some babies will actually settle themselves back to sleep.

Babies of this age may still be waking up in the night because they are getting out of their covers. Tuck the covers in using two rolled-up towels wedged between the mattress and the spars of the cot to keep the sheet firm.

By 4–5 months

If your babies reach five months and are still waking in the night, you probably need to persevere with their routine, paying increased attention to the timings of the feeds and the amount of daytime sleep they are getting (see page 163). If you feel that both or either of them are showing signs that they are ready to be weaned, consult your health visitor or GP for advice on whether they should begin earlier than the recommended six months (see Chapter 8 for more details).

Milk feeding chart for the first year

Age	Times
2–4 weeks	2–3am 6–6.45am 9.45–10.30am 1.45pm 4.45pm 5.45–6.45pm 9.45–10.45pm
4–6 weeks	3–4am 6–6.45am 9.45am 2/2.15pm 4.45pm 5.45pm 10–11pm
6–8 weeks	4–5am 6.45am 10.30–11.30am 2.15pm 5.45pm 10–11pm
8–12 weeks	5–6am 6.45am 10.30/10.45am 2–2.30pm 5.45pm 9.45/10.15pm
3–4 months	6.45am 10.45am 2/2.15pm 5.45pm 10pm
4–5 months	6.45am 10.45am 2/2.15pm 5.45pm 10pm
5–6 months	6.45am 10.45am 2/2.15pm 5.45pm
6–9 months	7am 2.30pm 6.20pm
9–12 months	7am 2.30pm 6.20pm

Structuring daytime sleep during the first year

To ensure good night-time sleep for your babies, it is essential that you structure their daytime sleep. Too much daytime sleep can result in night-time waking. Too little daytime sleep leads to overtired, irritable babies who have difficulty settling themselves to sleep, and who fall asleep only when totally exhausted. An exhausted baby will rarely feed well, so it is important to understand that the CLB routines are not just about the timings of feeds, but ensuring that the timings fit in with your babies' daily sleep requirements. The following guidelines will help you to ensure that this happens.

- By 3–4 months, most babies are capable of sleeping 12 hours at night with a quick last feed at 10pm, provided their daytime sleep is no more than three to three-and-a-half hours divided between two or three naps a day.
- If you want your babies to sleep from 7/7.30pm to 7/7.30am, it is very important that you structure these naps so that they have the longest one at midday, and two shorter ones – in the morning and late afternoon.

- While it may be more convenient to let your babies have a longer nap in the morning followed by a shorter nap in the afternoon, this can lead to problems as they get older.

Understanding the sleeping routine

Morning nap

During the first few weeks your babies will probably only manage to stay awake one to one-and-a-half hours from the time they wake up, and need to be settled between 8 and 8.30am for a nap of no longer than one to one-and-a-half hours. By the time they reach six weeks, they should show signs of being able to stay awake longer in the morning, settling between 8.30–9am. The important thing to remember is that they should stay awake no longer than two hours. Otherwise they could become overtired and not settle well, which would put your sleeping and feeding routine out for the rest of the day. Until a proper sleep pattern is established, try to ensure that this nap, whenever possible, takes place in the nursery in the dark.

Six weeks onwards

It is around this age that the babies should manage to stay awake until nearer 9am and by eight weeks should aim to have a nap of no more than 45 minutes. It is important that you start to wake the first baby around 9.30am, so that he is properly awake by 9.45am. If they are to sleep well at lunchtime they do need to be awake for a long enough spell during the second part of the morning. Keep a close eye on how long they are sleeping at lunchtime to ensure that when they are ready to cut back further on their total daytime sleep it happens at the morning nap. If by eight weeks they are still needing one-and-a-half hours sleep in the morning, I would suggest that you gradually try to extend the time that they are awake by two to three minutes every three to four days, so that they eventually can stay awake happily to 9am, therefore establishing a nap of no more than 45 minutes in the morning. This will help ensure that they continue to sleep well at the lunchtime nap, which should continue to be the longest nap of the day until they are well over the age of two years.

Six months onwards

Once your babies are on three meals a day, this nap may be pushed to 9.30am. You will know the babies are ready for this if either of them consistently chatters for 30 minutes or so when you put them down. This nap may need to be cut back to 20–30 minutes if they are sleeping less than two hours at lunchtime from 12 months onwards.

If they are awake at 6.45am, they may still need a short nap of 30 minutes at 9.30am. If you find they are sleeping for only 10–15 minutes of the 45-minute nap and are happily getting through to their lunchtime nap, you could cut it out altogether. If they sleep to 8am, they should be able to get through to the lunchtime nap without the morning nap.

Lunchtime nap

This should always be the longest nap of the day. By establishing a good lunchtime nap you will ensure that your babies are not too tired to enjoy afternoon activities and that bedtime is relaxed and happy. A nap between 11.30am and 2pm is deep and refreshing because it coincides with the babies' natural dip in alertness.

Most babies will need a sleep of two to two-and-a-half hours until they are two years of age, when it will gradually reduce to one to one-and-a-half hours. By three years of age they may not need a sleep after lunch, but they should always be encouraged to have some quiet time, otherwise they can get very hyperactive by late afternoon, which can affect the night sleep.

Six weeks onwards

If your babies are sleeping the full 45 minutes in the morning, they should be woken after two-and-a-quarter hours. If for some reason their morning nap is much shorter, you could allow them two-and-a-half hours. If either of your babies develops a problem with their night-time sleep, do not make the mistake of letting them sleep longer during the day.

In the early days a lunchtime nap may sometimes go wrong and your babies may wake early and refuse to go back to sleep. Obviously, they cannot happily make it through from 1pm to 4pm, so the best way to deal with this is to allow 30 minutes' sleep after the 2.30pm feed, then a further 30 minutes at 4.30pm. This should stop them getting overtired and irritable, and get things back on track so that they go to sleep well at 7pm.

Six months onwards

If your babies are on three meals a day, or you have moved the morning nap from 9am to 9.30am, they will most likely need the lunchtime nap adjusted to 12.30–2.30pm. If they are sleeping less than two hours at lunchtime, check that the morning nap is for no longer than 45 minutes.

Twelve months onwards

If either of your babies has difficulty in settling for the nap or is waking up after one to one-and-a-half hours, you might have to cut the morning nap right back or cut it out altogether. Do not let either baby sleep after 2.30pm if you want them to go to sleep at 7pm.

Late afternoon nap

This is the shortest nap of the three, and the one your babies should drop first. It is not essential that they go in the cot for this nap. In fact, it is a good idea to let them catnap in their buggy or chair at this time because it allows you the freedom to get out and about.

Three months onwards

If you want your babies to go to sleep at 7pm, they should never sleep more than 30 minutes at this nap, and they should both always be awake by 4.45pm regardless of how long or short their sleep was. Most babies who are sleeping well at the other two naps will gradually cut back on this sleep until they cut it out altogether. If for some reason the lunchtime nap is cut short, you need to allow them a short sleep in the late afternoon, but ensure that the daily total does not exceed the amount needed for their age.

Adjusting the routines

Birth to four months

The 7am to 7pm routine is the one in which I found tiny babies and young infants seem happiest. It fits in with their natural sleep rhythms and their need to feed little and often.

In the very early weeks, to avoid more than one waking in the night, you must fit in at least five to six feeds for each baby before midnight. This can only be done if your babies start the day near to 7am. An 8am to 8pm routine in the first few weeks means your babies would end up feeding twice between midnight and 7am.

Once your babies reach the age of four months, are on four feeds a day and need less sleep, it is possible to change the routine without affecting their natural needs for the right amount of sleep and number of feeds.

Four months onwards

From four months many babies will be capable of going through the night from 11pm to 6/7am. It is then easier to adjust the routine. If your babies have been sleeping regularly to 6.45am, it could be possible to change to a 7.00/7.30am start and push the rest of the routine forward. In this case, your babies would obviously need to go to sleep later in the evenings.

If you want your babies to sleep later in the mornings but still go to bed at 7pm, cut right back on the morning nap so that they are ready to go to bed at 12/12.30pm. Allow a nap of no longer than two hours at lunchtime, and no late afternoon nap.

Out and about

In the first few weeks, most young babies will go to sleep the minute they are in the car or the buggy. If possible, try to organise shopping trips during the sleep times so that the routine is not too disrupted. Once the routine is established and your babies are nearly eight weeks, you will find that you are able to go out more without them falling asleep the whole time.

If you are planning a day visit to friends, depending on the length of the visit, you can usually work it into the routine by travelling between 9am and 10am or 1pm and 2pm. By the time you arrive at the destination the babies will be due for a feed and can be kept awake. Likewise, by making the return journey between 4pm and 5pm or after 7pm you should manage to keep things on track.

Routines for twins during the first year | 7

'On your marks...' – Alice

I often wonder, if I had done the normal thing and produced a single child, would I have followed Gina's routines? I hope so. Two-and-a-half years down the line I am so comfortable with the way my girls eat, sleep and play. They are genuinely contented little children, and I know a big part of that is their routine. We can mess up their day on occasion for parties or visits, but know that the next day they will just fall back into place.

Before we first started the routines, we were all very tired and confused. The babies were sleeping, feeding, pooing and crying like all little things, but they just weren't settled and neither were we. With more than one baby, trying to do things on an ad hoc or on-demand basis was a game show from hell. You never knew when the 'hooter' was going to blow; you never knew how much time you had for anything, even a cup of tea. As soon as the routines fell into place, there was a noticeable release of tension in the house and we got on with enjoying every precious minute with our little ones . . . and each other too.

Once we all knew what we were doing, it was easier for us to anticipate the times of day when it was tricky without help, and the times when they would sleep and we could wash, eat or try to catch 40 winks ourselves. At first it seemed too good to be true: just when Gina said they would be ready for a nap at nine o'clock in the morning, blow me, they slept beautifully, allowing me to have a shower. In fact, all the naps worked immediately – and they still do.

The hardest part of any *CLB* routine, and the part that niggles at many older relatives, was waking them up at the advised time. There is something built in to anyone over 50 that you never ever wake a sleeping baby. Nonetheless, we converted even the most doubtful when they came to stay in the room next to the twins and heard not a peep between the hours of seven and seven. Without a doubt, if we had given in to the well-meaning advice of some people and left the babies to sleep all day in the early months, they would have been awake all night, long after the dispensers of wisdom had gone home and snuggled under their own duvets for the requisite eight hours. Getting the daytime sleep right did mean waking them at first when they seemed so sweetly asleep. Once the routines had been in place for a few weeks, however, we would go to wake them and find them waking up naturally, full of beans for the afternoon after a properly restful sleep. Catnapping did work at the very beginning, but as they got older and less sleepy, a proper long sleep in the middle of day was exactly what they needed. It meant they weren't tetchy mid-afternoon. They still have this nap and I know that it has helped them to enjoy their afternoons enormously. I'm also sure that the many things toddlers have to learn about the world around them are best absorbed by an alert and energetic child, rather than an overtired and grumpy one.

~

Alice's tip

There were occasions, even when we had started the routines, when both babies woke at the same time needing me. This is inevitable. At first I would hold them both and jig them around but really you just need to be prepared. I had a feed ready and a place on the sofa where I could give them a 10-minute feed together to calm them down. I found it better to try and attend to them both at once than try and calm one, then the other.

Routine for breast-feeding twins at two to four weeks

Feed times	Nap times between 7am and 7pm
6.45am	8.15–9.45am
9.45am	11.15am–1.45pm
1.45pm	3.45–4.45pm
4.45pm	
5.45–6.45pm	
9.45pm	

Maximum daily sleep 5 hours

6.45am
- **One of the twins should be awake, nappy changed and feeding no later than 6.45am.**
- Offer at least 15–20 minutes on the breast before starting to wake the second baby.
- When the first baby has fed (for 15–20 minutes), change the nappy of the second baby and start feeding.
- Once the second baby has fed for 15–20 minutes, go back and finish the feed of the first baby, then finish the feed of the second baby.

- **Do not feed after 7.45am as it will put them off the next feed.**
- They can stay awake for up to two hours, but no longer.

7.45am
- You should have cereal, toast and a drink no later than 7.45am.

8.15am
- The baby who awoke first should start to get a bit sleepy by this time. Check the nappy and draw sheet of the first baby, fully swaddle him (see page 26) and settle him in his cot.
- Always try to settle to sleep the baby who fed first at least 10–15 minutes before settling the second baby.

8.30am
- Close the curtains.
- Check the nappy and draw sheet of the second baby, fully swaddle him and settle him in his cot.
- **Both babies should be settled in their cots, fully swaddled and in the dark with the door shut, before they get into a deep sleep.**
- They need a sleep of no longer than one-and-a-half hours.

9.30am
- Open the curtains and unswaddle the first baby so that he can wake up naturally.
- Prepare things for top and tailing and dressing.

9.45am
- The first baby should be given 15–20 minutes on the breast while you drink a large glass of water, before unswaddling the second baby.
- Continue to feed the first baby until the second baby is fully awake.
- Once the second baby is fully awake, offer 15–20 minutes on the breast.
- Top and tail and dress the first baby, then offer the remainder of the feed.

- Top and tail and dress the second baby, then offer the remainder of the feed.
- Put both babies under the playgym or mobile so that they can have a good kick before they get too tired.
- **Do not feed after 11.00am as it will put them off the next feed.**

11.15am
- If the twins were very alert and awake during the previous two hours, they may start to get tired by 11.15am and need to be in bed by 11.30am.

11.30am
- Regardless of what they have done earlier, they should be taken to their room now.
- Check the draw sheets and change the babies' nappies, then close the blinds and curtains.
- Settle the first baby, fully swaddled, in the cot before fully swaddling and settling the second baby.
- **Both babies should be put in their cots before they get into a deep sleep, and no later than 11.45am.**

11.15/11.30am–1.45/2pm
- They need a nap of no longer than two-and-a-half hours from the time they went down.
- **If either wakes after 45 minutes, check the swaddling but do not talk or turn the lights on.**
- Allow 20 minutes for them to resettle themselves; if they are still unsettled, offer half the 1.45pm feed, and settle them back to sleep until 1.45pm.

12 noon
- Have lunch and rest before the next feed.

1.45pm
- Open the curtains and unswaddle the first baby. Once awake, offer 15–20 minutes on the breast before unswaddling the second baby.

- The second baby should be awake and feeding no later than 2pm. Offer 15–20 minutes on the breast.
- Change the nappy of the first baby and finish the feed, then change the nappy of the second baby and finish the feed.
- **Do not feed after 3.15pm as it will put them off the next feed.**
- **Very important: they should be fully awake until 3.45pm so that they go down well at 7pm.**

3.15pm
- If they get very irritable and unable to stay awake, let them have a catnap of no more than 15 minutes. They should be awake by 3.30pm.

3.30pm
- Change the babies' nappies. This is a good time to take them for a walk to ensure that they sleep well and are refreshed for their bath and next feed.

4.15pm
- If they are still awake and had a catnap earlier, it is essential that they have a further 15 minutes before 5pm, otherwise they will be overtired for their bath.

4.45pm
- **They should not sleep after 4.45pm if you want them to go down well at 7pm.**
- Offer the first baby 20 minutes on the breast, then offer the second baby the breast for 20 minutes.

5.20pm
- If they have been very awake during the day or didn't nap well between 4.15 and 4.45pm, they may need to start their bath early.
- Allow them both a good kick without their nappies while you prepare the bath and lay out things needed for bedtime.

5.30pm
- The one who woke first at 4.45pm must start his bath no later than 5.30pm, and be massaged and dressed by 5.45pm.

5.45pm
- The one who bathed first must start his feed no later than 5.45pm.
- Give him half his feed and put him in his chair.

6pm
- The second baby must start his bath no later than 6pm, and be massaged and dressed by 6.15pm.

6.15pm
- The second baby must start his feed no later than 6.15pm.
- Put the second baby in his chair, and give the first baby the rest of his feed.
- Fully swaddle the first baby and put him in his cot.

6.45pm
- Give the second baby the rest of his feed.
- Put him in his chair while you settle the first baby (if he has not fallen asleep already).

7pm
- Fully swaddle the second baby and settle him in his cot in the dark no later than 7pm. **This should be done in the nursery with dim lights and no talking or eye contact.**

9.45pm
- Turn on the lights fully and unswaddle the first baby so that he can wake up naturally. Once awake, allow at least 10 minutes before feeding to ensure he is fully awake and feeds well. This should be done before unswaddling the second baby.

- Lay out things for their nappy change, plus spare draw sheets, muslins and swaddle blankets in case they are needed in the middle of the night.
- Give the first baby most of his bottle-feed, then put him in his chair or on the floor on the playmat.
- By this time the second baby should be awake. Offer him most of his bottle-feed, then put him in his chair on the floor on the playmat.
- Change the nappy of the first baby, fully swaddle him, then finish his feed.
- Change the nappy of the second baby and fully swaddle him.
- Dim the lights and settle the first baby in his cot or Moses basket.
- With no talking or eye contact, give the second baby the remainder of his feed.
- This whole feed should take no more than one hour from start to finish.

In the night
- Make sure you keep the lights dim and avoid eye contact or talking. Change the babies' nappies only if really necessary.

Changes to be made during the two- to four-weeks routine

Sleeping

By 3–4 weeks your babies should start to show signs of being more wakeful and for longer periods. Ensure that you encourage this wakefulness during the day so that their night-time sleep is not adversely affected. If possible, continue to put them in their nursery in the dark with the door shut for all their daytime sleeps, except for the late afternoon one. If school runs with older children prevent this, try at least to put them down for their lunchtime nap in the nursery in the dark.

By four weeks the morning nap should have reduced to approximately one-and-a-quarter hours to ensure that the babies sleep well at lunchtime. Gradually aim to keep them awake longer in the morning, until they are going down for their sleep at 8.45am. If you find that they are going to sleep at 8.30am and waking up between 9.15 and 9.30am, which has an adverse affect on the rest of the day, topping and tailing them around 8.30am is usually enough to revive most babies so that they last until nearer 9am.

If the school run prevents you from doing this and the babies are awake from 9.15am, you could try allowing them a catnap of 10 minutes around 10.45/11am. This means that they would go down for their lunchtime nap somewhere between 12.15 and 12.30pm, avoiding the much earlier time of 11.15am if they had been awake since 9.15am. The lunchtime nap should be no more than two-and-a-half hours, and the afternoon nap no more than one hour in total. The latter is sometimes broken into a couple of catnaps between 4 and 5pm.

By four weeks the babies should be half-swaddled (under the arms) for the late afternoon nap. Around four weeks it becomes more obvious when they are coming into their light sleep, normally every 45 minutes, although it can be every 30 minutes with some babies. If a feed is not due, most babies, given the opportunity, settle themselves back to sleep. Rushing to your babies too quickly and assisting them back to sleep by rocking, patting or using a dummy could result in a long-term sleep association problem. This means that when your babies come into a light sleep in the night, you could be getting up several times to help them back to sleep, long after a time that they no longer need night feeds.

If you find that they are not settling themselves back to sleep after a short spell, you should, of course, assume that hunger is the cause and offer them a feed. But look closely at the daytime feeding to ensure that they are getting enough during the day at each feed, and particularly at the 10pm feed.

Feeding

Most babies go through a growth spurt around the third week. When your babies do this, reduce the amount that you express before their first feeds at 6.45/7am by 30ml (1oz). This will ensure that they immediately receive the extra milk they need. If you have not been expressing, you will have to allow them to feed for longer on the breast at feeds, and put them to the breast more often so that they get the extra milk they need. I would advise you to top up the babies before each daytime nap with a short breast-feed to ensure that they sleep well at naptimes and do not wake up early due to hunger. During this time it is very important that you try to get extra rest so that the babies' increased feeding demands do not cause you to become so exhausted that your milk supply decreases even further.

If you are breast-feeding and have decided to give one formula-feed a day, this is a good age to introduce it. If you leave it any later than this age, it is very possible that one or both of your babies will refuse a bottle altogether, which can cause enormous problems later on, particularly if you are going back to work.

To ensure that your breast milk does not decrease with the introduction of one formula-feed, it is advisable to express somewhere between 9.30 and 10pm. You must totally empty both breasts to keep up your milk supply. This milk can be used for the 9.45pm feed, or frozen and used on the occasions when you need to leave your babies with a sitter.

Introducing a bottle of either expressed milk or formula at 9.45pm also allows your partner to get involved, and enables you to go to bed earlier, giving you some extra sleep that you will most certainly need during the early weeks. If you wish to breast-feed for longer than six weeks, try to avoid giving formula at any other feeds unless advised to do so by your health visitor or paediatrician.

Formula-fed babies should have their 6.45/7am, 10/10.15am and 9.45pm feeds increased during growth spurts. Some bottle-fed babies are ready to move from a newborn teat to a slow-flow teat.

Once the babies reach four weeks, they will probably show signs of being happy to go slightly longer between feeds, and you should be able to move them onto the 4–6 weeks feeding routine, provided they are regularly gaining 180–240g (6–8oz) of weight each week. If they are breast-feeding and are not gaining this amount of weight each week, I would advise that they stay on the 2–4 weeks routine until their weight gain improves. Low weight-gain in breast-fed babies is usually caused by a low milk supply or poor positioning on the breast; in fact, the two usually go hand in hand. It would be worth giving them extra milk, in the form of a top-up feed just before nap times, to help increase your milk supply. I also advise you to arrange a home visit from a breast-feeding counsellor to check that you are positioning the babies correctly on the breast.

If you are feeding the babies together, it may be advisable to try feeding them separately for a week or so to ensure that they both are getting enough milk at each feed.

If the babies are formula-fed and not gaining sufficient weight, try moving them from the newborn teat with one hole to the slow-flow teat with two holes. However, always discuss any concerns you have about your babies' feeding or weight gain with your health visitor or paediatrician.

If you find that one or both of the babies is still waking around 2am, then again at 5am, despite making a good weight gain each week, I suggest that, at the 9.45pm feed, you wake them both up for a longer time than the recommended one hour and split the feed. Provided they are not sleeping excessively during the day, or waking up because they have kicked their covers off, having a split feed at this time and being awake for longer should help them manage to sleep nearer to 3am.

Routine for breast-feeding twins at four to six weeks

Feed times	Nap times between 7am and 7pm
6.45am	8.45–9.45am
9.45–10.15am	11.15/11.45am–1.45/2.15pm
2/2.15pm	4–4.45pm
4.45pm	
5.45pm	
10pm	

Maximum daily sleep 4½ hours

6.45am
- **One of the twins should be awake, nappy changed and feeding no later than 6.45am.**
- Offer at least 15–20 minutes on the breast before starting to wake the second baby.
- When the first baby has fed (for 15–20 minutes), change the nappy of the second baby and start feeding.
- Once the second baby has fed for 15–20 minutes, finish the feed of the first baby, then finish the feed of the second baby.
- **Do not feed after 7.45am as it will put them off the next feed.**
- They can stay awake for up to two hours, but no longer.

7.45am
- You should have cereal, toast and a drink no later than 7.45am.

8.30am
- The baby who woke first should start to get a bit sleepy by this time. Check the nappy and draw sheet of the first baby, fully or half-swaddle him and settle him in his cot.
- Always try to settle to sleep the baby who fed first at least 10–15 minutes before settling the second baby.

8.45am
- Close the curtains.
- Check the nappy and draw sheet of the second baby, fully or half-swaddle him and settle him in his cot.
- **Both babies should be settled in their cots, fully or half-swaddled and in the dark with the door shut, no later than 8.45am.**
- They need a sleep of no longer than one hour.

9.30am
- Open the curtains and unswaddle the first baby so that he can wake up naturally.
- Prepare everything needed for top and tailing and dressing.

9.45am
- Top and tail and dress the first baby.
- Unswaddle the second baby.
- The first baby should be given 15–20 minutes on the breast while you drink a large glass of water. This should allow time for the second baby to be fully awake.
- Top and tail and dress the second baby.
- Lay the first baby on his playmat so that he can have a good kick while you feed the second baby for 15–20 minutes.
- Lay the second baby on his playmat so that he can have a good kick while you offer the first baby the remainder of his feed.
- Lay the first baby on his playmat so that he can have a good kick while you offer the second baby the remainder of his feed.
- Lay the second baby on the playmat with the first baby.
- **Do not feed after 11.15am as it will put them off the next feed.**

11.15am
- If the twins were very alert during the previous two hours, they may start to get tired by 11.15am and need to be in bed by 11.30am.

11.30am

- Regardless of what they have done earlier, they should be taken to their room now.
- Check the draw sheets and change nappies, then close the blind and curtains.
- Settle the first baby fully or half-swaddled in the cot before fully or half swaddling and settling the second baby.
- **Both babies should be put in their cots before they get into a deep sleep, and no later than 11.45am.**

11.15/11.45–1.45/2.15pm

- They need a nap of no longer than two-and-a-half hours from the time they went down.
- **If either wakes after 45 minutes, check the swaddling but do not talk or turn on the lights.**
- Allow 20 minutes for them to resettle themselves; if they are still unsettled after 20 minutes, offer half the 2pm feed, and settle them back to sleep until 2.15pm.

12 noon

- Have lunch and rest before the next feed.

2pm

- Open the curtains and unswaddle the first baby. Once awake, offer 15–20 minutes on the breast before unswaddling the second baby.

2.30pm

- The second baby should be awake and feeding no later than 2.30pm. Offer him 15–20 minutes on the breast.
- Change the nappy of the first baby and finish his feed, then change the nappy of the second baby and finish the feed.
- **Do not feed after 3.15pm as it will put them off the next feed.**
- **Very important: try to keep the babies awake until nearer 4pm so that they go down well at 7pm.**
- Do not put too many clothes on them as extra warmth will make them drowsy.

- Lay the twins on their playmat and encourage them to have a good kick.

3.45pm
- Change the babies' nappies. This is a good time to take them for a walk to ensure they sleep well and are refreshed for their bath and next feed.
- The twins should not sleep after 4.45pm if you want them to go down well at 7pm.

4.45pm
- Offer the first baby 15–20 minutes on the breast.
- Put him in his chair or on the playmat.

5pm
- Offer the second baby the breast for 15–20 minutes.

5.20pm
- If they have been very awake during the day or didn't nap well between 3.45 and 4.45pm, they may need to start their bath early.
- Allow them both a good kick without their nappies while you prepare the bath and lay out things needed for bedtime.

5.30pm
- The one who woke first at 4.45pm must start the bath no later than 5.30pm, and be massaged and dressed by 5.45pm.

5.45pm
- The one who bathed first must start his feed no later than 5.45pm.
- Give him half his feed and put him in his chair.

6pm
- The second baby must start his bath no later than 6pm, and be massaged and dressed by 6.15pm.

6.15pm
- The second baby must start his feed no later than 6.15pm.
- Put the second baby in his chair, and give the first baby the rest of his feed.
- Fully or half-swaddle the first baby and put him in his cot.

6.45pm
- Give the second baby the rest of his feed.
- Put him in his chair while you settle the first baby (if he has not fallen asleep already).

7pm
- Fully or half-swaddle the second baby and settle him in his cot in the dark no later than 7pm. **This should be done in the nursery with dim lights and no talking or eye contact.**

9.45pm
- Turn on the lights fully and unswaddle the first baby so that he can wake up naturally. Once awake, allow at least 10 minutes before feeding to ensure he is fully awake and feeds well. This should be done before unswaddling the second baby.
- Lay out things for their nappy change, plus spare draw sheets, muslins and swaddle blankets in case they are needed in the middle of the night.

10pm
- Give the first baby most of his feed, then put him in his chair or on the floor on the playmat.
- By this time the second baby should be awake. Offer him most of his feed, then put him in his chair or on the floor on the playmat.
- Change the nappy of the first baby, fully or half-swaddle him, then finish his feed.
- Change the nappy of the second baby, and fully or half-swaddle him.
- **Dim the lights and settle the first baby in his cot or Moses basket.**

- With no talking or eye contact, give the second baby the remainder of his feed.
- This whole feed should take no more than one hour from start to finish.

In the night
- Make sure you keep the lights dim and avoid eye contact or talking. Change their nappies only if really necessary.

Changes to be made during the four-to-six-weeks routine

Sleeping

The babies' daily nap time between 7am and 7pm should be reduced to a strict four-and-a-half hours. The morning nap should be no more than one hour, and the afternoon nap no more than 45 minutes between 4pm and 5pm.

If either of the babies is very sleepy during the day and not managing to stay awake for the suggested times, see Chapter 4, page 83, to check if this could become a real problem.

It is very important that by the end of six weeks you start to get the babies used to being half-swaddled (under the arms) by half-swaddling them at the 9am and 7pm sleeps. Cot-death rates peak between two and four months, and overheating is considered to play a major part in this.

It should now take less time to settle the babies to sleep. The cuddling time should gradually be reduced, and now is a good time to get them used to going down when they are sleepy but still awake. Often a lullaby light, which plays a tune and casts images on the ceiling for 10 minutes or so, will help a baby to settle himself.

The babies should start to sleep a longer stretch in the night around now, provided they are getting most of their daily milk intake between 6/7am and 11.30pm. Their weight is a good indicator of this: they should regularly be gaining 180–240g

(6–8oz) each week. They also need to be staying awake for nearly two hours at their social time, although some twins who were very small at birth may manage to stay awake for only one-and-a-half hours after feeds. As long as they are not waking excessively in the night, this is not a problem; it just means that they need more sleep than I recommend. When they are ready they will manage to stay awake longer.

Once they have done a longer stretch in the night several nights in a row, try not to feed them if they suddenly go back to waking earlier again. The hours after the 10pm feed are sometimes referred to as the 'core night', and if the babies wake during these hours, you could follow the 'core night method'. This involves leaving them initially for a few minutes to settle themselves back to sleep. If that doesn't work, other methods, apart from feeding, should be used to settle them. I would try offering some cool boiled water or a cuddle, but others recommend a dummy. Attention should be kept to the minimum while reassuring the babies that you are there. This teaches them one of the most important sleep skills: how to nod off again after surfacing from a non-REM sleep. Obviously, if they refuse to settle, you should feed them, as the reason for the waking is probably genuine hunger.

The aim of the core night method is gradually to increase the length of time your babies can go from their last feed without eliminating the night feed in one go. Before embarking on this method, study the following points to make sure your baby really is capable of going for a longer spell in the night.

- Never use with very small babies or a baby who is not gaining weight. (A baby not gaining weight should always be seen by a doctor.)
- Use only if your babies are regularly gaining 180–240g (6–8oz) each week, and if you are sure that their last feed is substantial enough to help them sleep for a longer stretch in the night.
- The main sign that a baby is ready to cut down on a night feed is regular weight gain and a reluctance to feed or taking less at the 7am feed.

- If a baby has shown signs that he is capable of sleeping a longer stretch over three or four nights, the core night method can be used.

Feeding

If the babies are six weeks and feeding between 3am and 4am, and you have to wake them at 7am every morning, very gradually, and by a very small amount, cut back the amount of milk that they are taking in the night. This will have a knock-on effect of them drinking more during the day and less in the night, and eventually they will drop the middle-of-the-night feed altogether. It is very important not to cut back this feed too much or too fast as the babies could then start to wake up long before 6.45/7am, which would defeat the whole purpose of getting them to sleep through from 10pm to 7am.

Keep increasing the day feeds rather than the night feeds. Cut back on the first expressing of the day by a further 30ml (1oz) and by the end of the six weeks, cut out the 10.30am expressing altogether. Most babies are happy to wait longer after the 6.45/7am feed, so gradually keep pushing the 10am feed forward until 10.30am. The exception to this would be if one or both of the babies is still waking for a feed at 5am and having a top-up at 7.30am. It is unlikely that they would get through to 10.30am on having only a top-up at 7.30am, so continue to feed them at 10am until they are feeding between 6am and 7am. If they are feeding at 10am, you may find that you will have to offer a top-up just before the lunchtime nap to ensure that they sleep well.

Most babies will go through a second growth spurt at six weeks, and want to spend longer on the breast at some feeds. When this happens they may need a top-up before naps if you have not been expressing. Formula-fed babies should have the 6.45am, 10am and 5.45pm feeds increased during growth spurts. If they are not sleeping well at lunchtime during their growth spurt, it would be worth giving them a top-up before going down for their nap. Once they have done a week of uninterrupted midday naps, gradually cut back the top-up until you have eliminated it altogether.

Routine for breast-feeding twins at six to eight weeks

Feed times	Nap times between 7am and 7pm
6.45am	8.45–9.30am
10.30am	11.30/11.45am–2/2.15pm
2.15pm	4.15–4.45pm
5.45–6.45pm	
10pm	
Maximum daily sleep 4 hours	

6.45am
- **One of the twins should be awake, nappy changed and feeding no later than 6.45am.**
- Offer at least 15–20 minutes on the breast before starting to wake the second baby.
- When the first baby has fed (for 15–20 minutes), change the nappy of the second baby and start feeding.
- Once the second baby has fed for 15–20 minutes, finish the feed of the first baby, then finish the feed of the second baby.
- **Do not feed after 7.45am as it will put them off the next feed.**
- They can stay awake for up to two hours, but no longer.

7.45am
- You should have cereal, toast and a drink no later than 7.45am.

8am
- Wash and dress the first baby, remembering to cream all his creases and dry skin.
- Do the same with the second baby.

8.30am
- Check the nappy and draw sheet of the first baby, half-swaddle him and settle him in his cot.
- Always try to settle the baby who fed first at least 10–15 minutes before settling the second baby.

8.45am
- Close the curtains.
- Check the nappy and draw sheet of the second baby, half-swaddle him and settle him in his cot.
- **Both babies should be settled in their cots, half-swaddled and in the dark with the door shut, no later than 8.45am.**
- They need a sleep of no longer than 45 minutes.

9.30am
- Open the curtains and unswaddle the first baby so that he can wake up naturally.

9.45am
- The first baby should be fully awake now, regardless of how long he slept.
- If he had a full feed at 6.45am, he should last until 10.30am for his next feed. If he fed earlier, followed by a top-up at 7.15am, he may need to start this feed slightly earlier.
- Encourage him to have a good kick under the playgym.
- Unswaddle the second baby. When he is awake, lay him next to his twin for a good kick.

10.30am
- The first baby should be given 15–20 minutes on the breast while you drink a large glass of water.
- Lay the first baby on his playmat so that he can have a good kick while you feed the second baby for 15–20 minutes.
- Lay the second baby on his playmat so that he can have a good kick while you offer the first baby the remainder of his feed.

- Lay the first baby on his playmat so that he can have a good kick while you offer the second baby the remainder of his feed.
- Lay the second baby on the playmat with his twin.
- **Do not feed after 11.30am as it will put them off the next feed.**

11.30am
- Regardless of what they have done earlier, the babies should be taken to their room now.
- Check the draw sheets and change nappies, then close the blind and curtains.
- Settle the first baby half-swaddled in the cot, before half-swaddling and settling the second baby.
- **Both babies should be put in their cots before they get into a deep sleep, and no later than 11.45am.**

11.30/11.45am–2/2.15pm
- They need a nap of no longer than two-and-a-half hours from the time they went down.

12 noon
- Have lunch and rest before the next feed.

2.15pm
- Open the curtains, unswaddle the first baby and allow him to wake up naturally, regardless of how much he has slept. Once awake, change his nappy.
- Unswaddle the second baby.
- Offer the first baby 15–20 minutes on the breast.
- Put the first baby on the playmat and encourage him to have a good kick.

2.30pm
- The second baby should be awake now. Change his nappy and offer him 15–20 minutes on the breast.
- Offer the first baby the remainder of his feed.
- Put the first baby on the playmat and encourage him to have a good kick.

- Offer the second baby the remainder of his feed.
- Put the second baby on the playmat and encourage him to have a good kick.
- **Do not feed after 3.15pm as it will put them off the next feed.**
- **Very important: they should be fully awake until 4.15pm so that they go down well at 7pm.**
- Do not put too many clothes on them as extra warmth will make them drowsy.

4pm
- Change the babies' nappies.
- Offer them both a drink of cool boiled water or well-diluted juice no later than 4.15pm. (If, once your babies reach eight weeks, they refuse water, try them with water with a hint of peach juice.)
- This is a good time to take them for a walk to ensure they sleep well and are refreshed for their bath and next feed.
- The twins should not sleep after 4.45pm if you want them to go down well at 7pm.

4.45pm
- **The first baby should be fully awake now if you want him to go down well at 6.45pm.**
- If the first baby is very hungry, offer him 15 minutes on the breast; otherwise try to make him wait until after his bath for a full feed. By eight weeks he should be able to achieve this.
- Put him on the playmat.

5pm
- **The second baby should be fully awake now if you want him to go down well at 7pm.**
- If the second baby is very hungry, offer him 15 minutes on the breast; otherwise try to make him wait until after his bath for a full feed. By eight weeks he should be able to achieve this.

5.20pm

- Allow them both a good kick without their nappies while you prepare the bath and lay out things needed for bedtime.

5.30pm

- The one who woke first at 4.45pm must start his bath no later than 5.30pm, and be massaged and dressed by 5.45pm.

5.45pm

- The one who bathed first must start his feed no later than 5.45pm.
- Give him half his feed, then put him in his chair.

6pm

- The second baby must start his bath no later than 6pm, and be massaged and dressed by 6.15pm.

6.15pm

- The second baby must start his feed no later than 6.15pm.
- Put the second baby in his chair, and give the first baby the rest of his feed.
- Half-swaddle the first baby and put him in his cot.

6.45pm

- Give the second baby the rest of his feed.
- Put him in his chair while you settle the first baby (if he has not fallen asleep already).

7pm

- Half-swaddle the second baby and settle him in his cot in the dark no later than 7pm. **This should be done in the nursery with dim lights and no talking or eye contact.**

9.45/10.15pm

- Turn on the lights fully and unswaddle the first baby so that he can wake up naturally. Once awake, allow at least 10 minutes before feeding to ensure he is fully awake and feeds well. This should be done before unswaddling the second baby.

- Lay out things for their nappy change, plus spare draw sheets, muslins and swaddle blankets in case they are needed in the middle of the night.
- Give the first baby most of his bottle-feed, then put him in his chair or on the floor on the playmat.
- By this time the second baby should be awake. Offer him most of his bottle-feed, then put him in his chair or on the floor on the playmat.
- Change the nappy of the first baby, half-swaddle him, then finish his feed.
- Change the nappy of the second baby and half-swaddle him.
- **Dim the lights and settle the first baby in his cot or Moses basket.**
- **With no talking or eye contact, give the second baby the remainder of his feed.**
- **This whole feed should take no more than one hour from start to finish.**

In the night
- Make sure you keep the lights dim and avoid eye contact or talking. Change their nappies only if really necessary.

Changes to be made during the six-to-eight-weeks routine

Sleep

Most babies who weigh over 4kg (9lb) should be sleeping longer in the night now, provided they are getting most of their daily nutritional needs between 6/7am and 11pm. They should also be sleeping no more than four hours between 7am and 7pm. Once they have lasted longer for several nights in a row, try not to feed your babies before that time again. The morning nap should be no more than 45 minutes, the lunchtime nap should be two-and-a-quarter to two-and-a-half hours (no longer), and the afternoon nap should be no more than 30 minutes. They may catnap on and off during this nap, but some babies cut out this nap altogether. Do not allow them to cut out this nap if they are not managing to stay awake until 7pm. If you want them to sleep until 7am, it is important that they go to sleep near 7pm. If for some reason the lunchtime nap went wrong, they may need slightly more sleep after the 2pm feed. Some babies will have a catnap of about 15 minutes after the 2pm feed at around 3pm, then a further catnap around 4.30/5pm.

By the end of eight weeks they should not be half-swaddled at the 9am, midday and 7pm sleeps, nor from 11pm to 7am. Some babies may start to wake up earlier in the night again once they are out of the swaddle; try to settle them without feeding or re-swaddling.

Feeding

If your babies go back to waking up earlier again, wait 10 minutes or so before going to them. If they will not settle themselves back to sleep, try settling them with some water or a cuddle. However, if they do not settle back quickly, you should assume that hunger is the cause and offer them enough milk to settle them back to sleep. The important thing is that they are asleep at this time, and not awake for any length of time because you are trying to get them to 7am without a feed.

Keep increasing daytime feeds rather than night feeds. Most babies are happy to wait longer after the 7am feed, so keep pushing this feed forward until they are feeding at 10.45am. However, if your babies are still feeding at 5/6am with a top-up at 7/7.30am, they may not manage to go longer, and need to have at least half of their next feed at 10am. Most babies go through a second growth spurt at six weeks. Cut back on the first expressing of the day by a further 30ml (1oz), and by the end of eight weeks cut out the 6.45am expressing so that your babies get the extra milk they need. They may also need to spend longer on the breast at some feeds during growth spurts.

Bottle-fed babies should have the 6.45am, 10.30am and 5.45pm feeds increased first during growth spurts. The 10pm feed should be increased only if all the other feeds have been increased, and if they are not going a longer spell in the night. Try not to give more than 180ml (6oz) at this feed. Some babies will need to move to a medium-flow teat with three holes at this stage.

Routine for breast-feeding twins at eight to twelve weeks

Feed times	Nap times between 7am and 7pm
6.45am	8.45–9.45am
10.30/10.45am	11.45am–2pm
2–2.30pm	4.30–4.45pm
5.45pm	
9.45/10.15pm	

Maximum daily sleep 3¼ hours

6.45am
- **One of the twins should be awake, nappy changed and feeding no later than 6.45am.**
- Offer at least 15–20 minutes on the breast before starting to wake the second baby.
- When the first baby has fed (for 15–20 minutes), change the nappy of the second baby and start feeding.
- Once the second baby has fed for 15–20 minutes, finish the first baby's feed, then finish the second baby's.

- **Do not feed after 7.45am as it will put them off the next feed.**
- They can stay awake for up to two hours, but no longer.

7.45am
- You should have cereal, toast and a drink no later than 7.45am.

8am
- Wash and dress the first baby, remembering to cream all his creases and dry skin.
- Do the same with the second baby.

8.30am
- Check the nappy and draw sheet of the first baby, half-swaddle him and settle him in his cot.
- Always try to settle the baby who fed first at least 10–15 minutes before settling the second baby.

8.45am
- Close the curtains.
- Check the nappy and draw sheet of the second baby, half-swaddle him and settle him in his cot.
- **Both babies should be settled in their cots, half-swaddled and in the dark with the door shut, no later than 8.45am.**
- They need a sleep of no longer than 45 minutes.

9.30am
- Open the curtains and unswaddle the first baby so that he can wake up naturally.

9.45am
- The first baby should be fully awake now, regardless of how long he slept.
- If he had a full feed at 6.45am, he should last until 10.30am for his next feed. If he fed earlier, followed by a top-up at 7.15am, he may need to start this feed slightly earlier.

- Encourage him to have a good kick under the playgym.
- Unswaddle the second baby. When he is awake, lay him next to his twin for a good kick.

10.30/10.45am
- The first baby should be given 15–20 minutes on the breast while you drink a large glass of water.
- Lay the first baby on his playmat so that he can have a good kick while you feed the second baby for 15–20 minutes.
- Lay the second baby on the playmat so that he can have a good kick while you offer the first baby the remainder of his feed.
- Lay the first baby on the playmat so that he can have another good kick while you offer the second baby the remainder of his feed.
- Lay the second baby on the playmat with his twin.
- **Do not feed after 11.30am as it will put them off the next feed.**

11.40am
- Regardless of what they have done earlier, they should be taken to their room now.
- Check the draw sheets and change nappies, then close the blind and curtains.
- Settle the first baby half-swaddled in the cot, before half-swaddling and settling the second baby.
- **Both babies should be put in their cots before they get into a deep sleep, and no later than 11.45am.**

11.45am–2pm
- They need a nap of no longer than two-and-a-quarter hours from the time they went down.

12 noon
- Have lunch and rest before the next feed.

2pm

- Open the curtains, unswaddle the first baby and allow him to wake up naturally, regardless of how much he has slept. He must be feeding no later than 2.30pm.
- Once awake, change his nappy.
- Unswaddle the second baby.
- Offer the first baby 15–20 minutes on the breast.
- Put the first baby on the playmat and encourage him to have a good kick.

2.30pm

- The second baby should be awake now. Change his nappy and offer him 15–20 minutes on the breast.
- Offer the first baby the remainder of his feed.
- Put the first baby on the playmat and encourage him to have a good kick.
- Offer the second baby the remainder of his feed.
- Put the second baby on the playmat and encourage him to have a good kick.
- **Do not feed after 3.15pm as it will put them off the next feed.**
- **Very important: they should be fully awake until 4.15pm so that they go down well at 7pm.**
- Do not put too many clothes on them as extra warmth will make them drowsy.

4pm

- Change the babies' nappies.
- Offer them both a drink of cool boiled water or well-diluted juice no later than 4.15pm. This is a good time to take them for a walk to ensure they sleep well and are refreshed for their bath and next feed.
- The twins may have a 15-minute nap between 4.30 and 4.45pm.
- They should not sleep after 4.45pm if you want them to go down well at 6.45pm.

4.45pm
- **The first baby should be fully awake now if you want him to go down well at 6.45pm.**
- He should be happy to wait until after the bath for his feed.
- Put him on the playmat.

5pm
- The second baby should be fully awake now if you want him to go down well at 7pm.
- He should be happy to wait until after the bath for his feed.
- Put him on the playmat.

5.20pm
- Allow them both a good kick without their nappies while you prepare the bath and lay out things needed for bedtime.

5.30pm
- The one who woke first at 4.45pm must start the bath no later than 5.30pm, and be massaged and dressed by 5.45pm.

5.45pm
- The one who bathed first must start his bottle-feed no later than 5.45pm.
- Give him half his bottle-feed and put him in his chair.

6pm
- The second baby must start his bath no later than 6pm, and be massaged and dressed by 6.15pm.

6.15pm
- The second baby must start his bottle-feed no later than 6.15pm.
- Put the second baby in his chair, and give the first baby the rest of his bottle-feed.
- Half-swaddle the first baby and put him in his cot.

6.45pm
- Give the second baby the rest of his bottle-feed.
- Put him in his chair while you settle the first baby (if he has not fallen asleep already).

7pm
- Half-swaddle the second baby and settle him in his cot in the dark no later than 7pm.

9.45pm
- Turn on the lights fully and unswaddle the first baby so that he can wake up naturally. Once awake, allow at least 10 minutes before feeding to ensure he is fully awake and feeds well. This should be done before unswaddling the second baby.
- Lay out everything for their nappy change, plus spare draw sheets, muslins and swaddle blankets in case they are needed in the middle of the night.
- Give the first baby most of his bottle-feed, then put him in his chair or on the floor on the playmat.
- By this time the second baby should be awake. Offer him most of his bottle-feed, then put him in his chair or on the floor on the playmat.
- Change the nappy of the first baby, fully swaddle him, then finish his feed.
- Change the nappy of the second baby and fully swaddle him.
- **Dim the lights and settle the first baby in his cot or Moses basket.**
- **With no talking or eye contact give the second baby the remainder of his feed.**
- **This whole feed should take no more than one hour from start to finish.**

In the night
- Make sure you keep the lights dim and avoid eye contact or talking. Change their nappies only if really necessary.

Changes to be made during the eight-to-twelve-weeks routine

Sleep

Most babies who weigh nearly 5.4kg (12lb) can manage to go through the night from the 10/11pm feed at this age, provided they are taking all their daily nutritional needs between 7am and 11pm. A totally breast-fed baby may still be waking up once in the night, hopefully near 5/6am.

Cut back your babies' daily nap time by a further 30 minutes to a total of three hours. The morning nap should be no more than 45 minutes, but if they are not sleeping so well at lunchtime, it can be cut back to 30 minutes. The lunchtime nap should be no more than two-and-a-quarter hours. It is around this stage that the lunchtime nap can sometimes go wrong. The babies come into a light sleep usually 30–45 minutes after they have gone to sleep. Some will wake fully and it is important that they learn how to settle themselves back to sleep if the wrong sleep associations are to be avoided. For more about this problem, see Chapter 4, page 76.

By this stage, most babies have cut out their late-afternoon nap, but if this is not so with your twins, do not allow them more than 15 minutes, unless for some reason the lunchtime nap has gone wrong, in which case you can give them slightly longer. All babies should be only half-swaddled and sleeping in their big cots.

Pay particular attention when tucking the babies into their cots. One reason many of them wake up is because they move around the cot and get their arms and legs caught in between the spars. If this is happening with your babies, I suggest you purchase a couple of 0.5tog summer-weight sleeping bags. They are so light that you can still use a sheet and one blanket to tuck them in without the worry of overheating. For further information about cots and bedding, see Chapter 1, pages 8–11.

Feeding

The twins should be well established on five feeds a day now, eventually taking a very small feed at 1pm. If they are totally breast-fed and have started waking up earlier in the morning, it may be worth trying a top-up from a bottle of either expressed or formula milk after you feed them at 10pm. If they are sleeping regularly to 6.45am, gradually bring the 10.30/11pm feed forward by five minutes every three nights until they are feeding at 10pm. As long they continue to sleep through to 6.45am and take a full feed, you can keep taking the 10.45am feed back until they are feeding at 11am.

If you are considering introducing a further bottle-feed, the best time to do so is at the 11am feed. Gradually reduce the time of the feed by two or three minutes each day and top up with formula. By the end of the first week, if your babies are taking a bottle-feed of 150–180ml (5–6oz), you should be able to drop the breast-feed easily without the risk of serious engorgement. Bottle-fed babies should continue to have their 6.45am, 10.30/10.45am and 5.45pm feeds increased first during the next growth spurt at around nine weeks. Increase the bottle-feed to suit your babies' needs.

Routine for twins at three to four months

Feed times	Nap times between 7am and 7pm
6.45am	9am–9.45am
10.45am	12 noon–2/2.15pm
2/2.15pm	4.30pm–4.45pm
5.45pm	
10pm	

Maximum daily sleep 3 hours

6.45am
- **One of the twins should be awake, nappy changed and feeding no later than 6.45am.**
- Offer him most of his breast-feed, before starting to wake the second baby.
- Change the second baby's nappy, and start feeding him.
- Once the second baby has had most of his feed, go back and finish the feed of the first baby, then finish the feed of the second baby.
- Do not feed the babies after 7.45am, as it will put them off their next feed.
- They can stay awake for up to two hours, but no longer.

8am
- They should be encouraged to have a good kick on their play mat for 20-30 minutes.
- Wash and dress both babies, remembering to cream all their creases and dry skin.

9am
- **Settle both babies, half-swaddled in their cots and in the dark with the door shut, no later than 9am.**
- Always try to settle the one who woke and fed first, to sleep 5-10 minutes before settling the second one.
- They need a sleep of between 30 –45 minutes.

9.45am
- Open the curtains slightly and unswaddle the first baby so that he can wake up naturally.
- Allow 5-10 minutes then unswaddle the second baby and allow him to wake up naturally.

10am
- **Both babies must be fully awake now regardless of how long they slept.**
- Encourage both of them to have a good kick under the play gym.

10.45am
- The baby who woke and fed first should have his nappy changed and be offered most of his feed.
- Change the second baby's nappy and then offer him most of his feed, then go back and finish the feed of the first baby, then finish the feed of the second baby.
- Do not feed after 11.30am, as will put them off their next feed

11.45am
- They should be taken to their room now.
- Change the babies' nappies, then close the blinds and the curtains.
- Settle the first baby, half-swaddled in the cot, before half-swaddling and settling the second baby.
- **Both babies should be put into their cots before they get into a deep sleep, and no later than 12 noon.**

12 noon-2/2.15pm
- Both babies need a nap of no longer than two-and-a-quarter hours from the time they went down.

2/2.15pm
- Open the curtains, unswaddle the first baby and allow him to wake up naturally, then change his nappy.
- Give him most of his feed, then unswaddle the second baby, allowing him to wake up naturally.
- Change the second baby's nappy and give him most of his feed, then go back and finish the first baby's feed, then finish the second baby's feed.
- **Do not feed them after 3.15pm as it will put them off their next feed.**
- **Very important: they should be fully awake until 4.30pm so that they go down well at 7pm.**

4.15pm
- Change the babies' nappies.
- Offer them both a drink of cool boiled water or well-diluted juice no later than 4.30pm.
- The twins may need a short nap of 15 minutes but they should not sleep after 4.45pm, if you want them to go down well at 7pm.

5pm
- Both babies should be happy to wait until after the bath for their feed, if they have had a small drink of water or well-diluted juice. If either of them is showing signs of hunger, then offer them a small feed before the bath.

5.20pm
- Allow them both a good kick without their nappies while you prepare the bath and lay out things needed for bedtime.

5.30pm
- The one who woke first at 4.45pm must start his bath no later then 5.30pm, and be massaged and dressed by 5.45pm. Give him most of his feed, and put him in his chair.

6pm
- The second baby must start his bath no later than 6pm, and be massaged and dressed no later than 6.15pm.

6.15pm
- Give the second baby most of his feed, then put him his chair while you give the first baby the rest of his feed.
- Burp the first baby and settle him in his cot with a book or toy to look at.
- Give the second baby the rest of his feed, burp him and settle him in his cot with a book or toy to look at.
- Dim the lights while you tidy up the nursery

7pm
- **Both babies should be settled in their cots, in the dark with the door shut, no later than 7pm.**

10pm
- Turn the lights on low and wake the first baby enough to feed him. Give him as much of his feed as he will take, burp him and lay him in his cot.
- Wake up the second baby just enough to feed him. Give him as much of his feed as he will take, burp him and lay him in his cot.
- Change the first baby's nappy, offer him a further feed then burp him and settle him back in his cot. Change the second baby's nappy and offer him a further feed, burp him well and settle him back in his cot.
- **This feed should be done with the lights dim, and with no talking or eye contact, if the babies are to settle back to sleep within one hour.**

Changes to be made during the three-to-four-month routine

Sleeping

If you have structured the milk feeds and naptimes according to the routine, your babies should manage to sleep through the night from their last feed to nearer 6-7am. If either of them shows signs of starting to wake up earlier it would be advisable to assume that it may be hunger and increase his 10pm feed and, if need be, go back to having him awake longer at that feed. You should also ensure that their maximum daily sleep between 7am and 7pm totals no more than three hours. Most babies will cut right back on their late afternoon sleep and some days may manage to get through the afternoon without the nap, but may need to go to bed 5-10 minutes earlier on those days.

If for some reason either of the babies has slept less than two hours at lunchtime they should certainly be encouraged to have a short nap of no longer than 30 minutes between 4 and 5pm, otherwise they may become so overtired at bedtime that they don't settle to sleep easily.

The time your babies are awake at the 10pm feed should gradually be reduced to 30 minutes, provided they are sleeping through regularly to 6.45am. This feed should be a very quiet feed, and treated like a middle-of-the-night feed. If either of them is still waking up between 5 and 6am it would be advisable to try and keep him awake for a least an hour at the last feed.

Even if they are not getting out of their half-swaddle I would suggest that now is a good time to get them used to a 100 per cent cotton very lightweight sleeping bag. They would still need to be tucked in firmly, with one sheet, and perhaps one blanket, depending on the room temprature; therefore it is important that your purchase a 0.5tog weight bag to avoid the risk of over-heating.

Feeding

If the babies are formula-fed and taking 1050 – 1200ml (35–40oz) of formula between 7am and 11pm, they should not really need to feed in the night. However, some very big babies who weigh over 6.8kg (15lb) at this stage may still need to feed between 5–6am, followed by a top-up at 7–7.30am until they reach six months and are weaned. Current guidelines are that babies are not weaned before six months. If you are concerned that either of your babies is showing signs of needing to be weaned, it is important that you discuss it with your health visitor or doctor.

It is better to keep feeding in the night for a slightly longer time than take the risk of weaning your babies before they are ready. A totally breast-fed baby may also need to feed around 5–6am as he may not be getting enough to eat at the last feed. Regardless of whether they are breast or bottle fed, a good indicator of whether either of your babies is ready to drop the night feed is how they take their top-up at 7–7.30am. If they take it greedily they are probably genuinely hungry at 5–6am. If they fuss and fret and refuse the top-up I would assume the early wake-up was more habit than hunger and try to settle them back with some cool boiled water or a cuddle.

If your babies continue to sleep through to 7am once their waking time at 10.30pm has been reduced to 30 minutes, plus they are cutting back on the 7am feed, start reducing the amount they are drinking at 10.30pm. Only continue with this if they are sleeping well until 7am. However, I would not advise dropping this feed altogether until they reach six months and solids have been introduced. If you abandon the 10.30pm feed before solids are introduced and they go through a growth spurt, you may find that you have to go back to feeding them in the middle of the night again.

If your babies are totally breast-fed, and weigh over 6.3kg(14lb) in weight, you may find that during growth spurts that you have to go back to feeding them in the middle of the night anyway, until solids are introduced.

Routine for twins at four to six months

Feed times	Nap times between 7am and 7pm
6.45am	9am–9.45am
10.45am	12.15pm–2/2.15pm
2.30pm	
5.45pm	
10pm	

Maximum daily sleep 3 hours

6.45am

- **One of the twins should be awake, nappy changed and feeding no later than 6.45am.**
- Offer him most of his breast-feed, before starting to wake the second baby.
- Change the second baby's nappy and start feeding him.
- Once the second baby has had most of his feed, go back and finish the feed of the first baby, then finish the feed of the second baby.
- Do not feed after 7.45am, as it will put them off their next feed.
- They can stay awake for up to two hours.

8am

- They should be encouraged to have a good kick on their play mat for 20-30 minutes.
- Wash and dress both babies, remembering to cream all their creases and dry skin.

9am

- **Settle both babies, half swaddled in their cots and in the dark with the door shut, no later than 9am.**
- Always try to settle the one who woke and fed first, to sleep 5-10 minutes before settling the second one
  They need a sleep of between 30 – 45 minutes

9.45am

- Open the curtains and unswaddle the first baby so that he can wake up naturally.
- Allow 5-10 minutes then unswaddle the second baby and allow him to wake up naturally.

10am

- Both babies must be fully awake now, regardless of how long they slept.
- Encourage both of them to have a good kick under the play gym.

10.45am
- The baby who woke and fed first should have his nappy changed and be offered most of his feed.
- Change the nappy of the second baby and then offer him most of his feed, then go back and finish the feed of the first baby, then finish the feed of the second baby
- **Do not feed after 11.30am, as this will put them off their next feed.**

11.45am
- They should be taken to their room now.
- Change nappies, then close the blinds and curtains.
- Settle the first baby half-swaddled in the cot, before half-swaddling and settling the second baby
- **Both babies should be settled in their cots before they get into a deep sleep, and no later than 12 noon**

12 noon-2/2.15pm
- Both babies need a nap of no longer than two-and-a-quarter hours from the time they went down.

2/2.15pm
- Open the curtains, unswaddle the first baby and allow him to wake up naturally, then change his nappy.
- Give him most of his feed, then unswaddle the second baby allowing him to wake up naturally.
- Change the second baby's nappy and give him most of his feed, then go back and finish the feed of the first baby, then finish the feed of the second baby
- **Do not feed them after 3.15pm as it will put them off the next feed.**
- **Very important: they should be fully awake now until 4.30pm, so that they go down well at 7pm.**

4.15pm
- Change the babies' nappies.
- Offer them both a drink of cool boiled water or well-diluted juice no later than 4.30pm.

- The twins may need a short nap of 15 minutes but should not sleep after 4.45pm, if you want them to go down well at 7pm

5pm
- Both babies should be happy to wait until after the bath for their feed if they have had a small drink of water or well-diluted juice. If either of them is showing signs of hunger, then offer a small feed before the bath.

5.20pm
- Allow them both a good kick without their nappies while you prepare the bath and lay out things needed for bedtime.

5.30pm
- The one who woke first must start his bath no later then 5.30pm, and be massaged and dressed by 5.45pm.
- Give him most of his feed, and put him in his chair.

6pm
- The second baby must start his bath no later than 6pm, and be massaged and dressed no later than 6.15pm.

6.15pm
- Give the second baby most of his feed, then put him in his chair while you give the first baby the rest of his feed.
- Burp the first baby, and settle him in his cot with a book or toy to look at.
- Give second baby the rest of his feed, burp him and settle him in his cot with a book or toy to look at.
- Dim the lights while you tidy up the nursery.

7pm
- **Both babies should be settled in their cots, in the dark with the door shut, no later than 7pm.**

10pm

- Turn the lights on low and wake the first baby enough to feed him. Give him as much of his feed as he will take, burp him and settle him in his cot.
- Wake up the second baby enough to feed him, give him as much of his feed as he will take, burp him and settle him in his cot.
- Change the first baby's nappy, offer him a further feed then burp him and settle him back in his cot.
- Change the second baby's nappy and offer him a further feed, burp him and settle him back in his cot.
- **This feed should be done with the lights dim, and with no talking or eye contact, if the babies are to settle back to sleep well within one hour.**

Changes to be made during the four-to-six-months routine

Sleep

Between four and six months your babies should manage to sleep from their last feed at 10pm until 6/7am in the morning, providing they are taking four to five full milk feeds a day, and not sleeping more than 3 hours between 7pm and 7am. If you have not already introduced a sleeping bag it would be advisable to do so at this stage. To leave it any later you may risk the problem of them being unhappy when they are eventually put into one. Until they are able to crawl and manoeuvre themselves around the cot, they need to be tucked in firmly. In very hot weather they can be put into their bags with just a nappy on and a very thin cotton sheet. If they are not sleeping the full two hours at lunchtime, cut back their morning nap to 20–30 minutes, and offer them a top-up of milk just before they go down for their lunch time nap.

Feeding

I would recommend that you continue to feed them both at 10pm until solids are introduced. The current guidelines are that solids should now be introduced at six months, rather than at four months as previously recommended. As your babies will continue to grow through growth spurts between four and six months, their nutritional needs will still have to be met. In my experience this can rarely be done on four milk feeds a day. If you do decide to drop the 10pm feed and one or both of the babies starts to wake up earlier and not settle back to sleep quickly, then you should assume that it is hunger and feed them. It would also be worth considering introducing the 10pm feed again until solids are introduced.

If you find that one or both of the babies are refusing their first feed of the day and being difficult about most of their other feeds during the day, then that would be a sign that the 10pm feed should be abandoned.

During growth spurts you may find that your babies are not content on five feeds a day. If this happens I would advise that you bring the 11am feed back to 10am, then top them up with a further feed at 11.30am. You may also have to re-introduce the 5pm feed again, if they are getting very fractious before the bath.

If your babies become very discontent between feeds, despite offering them extra milk, and you think that they are showing signs of needing to be weaned, then it is important that you discuss this with your health visitor or doctor. If they advise that your babies do need to be weaned before six months, then it is important that you introduce solids very carefully. Solids should only be seen as tasters and given in addition to milk at this stage, not to replace milk feeds.

To ensure that this does not happen always make sure that your babies take all of their milk feed first. Start off with a small amount of baby rice mixed with either breast milk or formula after the 11am feed. Once the babies are taking this you can then transfer the rice to after the 6pm feed, then start to introduce some of the first weaning foods recommended on page 000.

If you find that the babies are getting too tired to have all of their milk at 6pm followed by the solids, then give them two-thirds of the milk at 5.15pm, followed by the solids, followed by the remainder of their milk at 6.45pm.

Once solids are introduced at this feed, and as they increase, they should automatically cut back on their last feed at 10pm. Once they are down to taking only a very short breast-feed or just a couple of ounces of formula at 10pm, but are still sleeping through until 7am, you should be able to drop the 10pm feed without any risk of them waking earlier in the morning.

Routine for twins at six to nine months

Feed times	Nap times between 7am and 7pm
7am	9/9.30am–9.45am
11–11.45am	12.30pm–2.30pm
2.30pm	
5pm	
6pm	

Maximum daily sleep 3 hours

7am
- **Babies should be awake, nappies changed and feeding no later than 7am.**
- They should have most of their milk feed, followed by breakfast cereal, mixed with either expressed milk or formula and fruit.
- They can stay awake for between two to two-and-a-half hours.

8am

- They should be encouraged to have a good kick on their play mat for 20-30 minutes.
- Wash and dress both babies, remembering to cream all their creases and dry skin.

9–9.30am

- **Settle both babies, in their cot in the dark with the door shut, between 9am and 9.30am.**
- They need a nap of 30 - 45 minutes.

9.30/9.45am

- Open the curtains and open their sleeping bags so that they can wake up naturally.

10am

- **Babies must be fully awake now, regardless of how long they slept.**
- Encourage them to have a good kick under their playgym or take them on an outing.

11am

- They should be given half of their milk, and then their solids followed by the remainder of their milk.
- Encourage them to sit in their chairs while you clear away the lunch things.

12.00–12.15pm

- Change the babies' nappies, and settle them in their sleeping bags in the dark with the door shut no later than 12.30pm.

12.30pm–2.30pm

- **They will need a nap now of no longer than two hours from the time they went down.**
- If they slept the full 45 minutes earlier, they may need less sleep at this nap.

2.30pm
- **Babies must be awake and feeding no later than 2.30pm regardless of how long they have slept.**
- Open the curtains, unzip their sleeping bags and allow them to wake up naturally. Change their nappies.
- They need a feed from both breasts or a full bottle feed.
- **Do not feed them after 3.15pm as it will put them off their next feed.**

4.15pm
- Change the babies' nappies and offer them a drink of cool boiled water or well-diluted juice no later than 4.30pm.

5pm
- They should be given most of their solids before being offered a small drink of water from a cup. It is important that they still have a good milk feed at bedtime, so keep this drink to a minimum.

5.45pm
- Put the babies on their changing mats on the floor without their nappies, so that they can have a good kick while you prepare their bath.

6pm
- They must start their bath no later than 6pm, and be massaged and dressed no later than 6.20pm.

6.20pm
- **Babies should be feeding no later than 6.20pm in a dimly lit room**
- Dim the lights and sit the babies in their chairs for ten minutes or in their cots with a toy or book to look at while you tidy up.

7pm
- **Settle the drowsy babies in their cots and in the dark with the door shut, no later than 7pm.**

Changes to be made during the six-to-nine-months routine

Sleep

Once your twins are established on three meals a day, they should manage to sleep from around 7pm to 7am. If you have followed the most recent guidelines on weaning and started weaning your baby on to solids at six months they will probably need a small feed at 10pm until they are nearer seven months. If you are advised to wean them before six months and solids are well established when they reach six months, you should be able to drop the 10pm feed sooner.

Once they reach six months and provided they are sleeping soundly to 7am most mornings, you should aim to keep pushing the 9am nap forward to 9.30am. This will encourage them to go down later for their lunchtime nap nearer to 12.30pm. This is important once solids are established and they are having three proper meals a day, with lunch coming around 11.45/12noon.

Some babies are happy to sleep later in the morning once they are established on three solid meals a day. If your babies sleep until nearer 8am, they will not need a morning nap, but may not manage to get through until 12.30pm for their lunchtime nap, therefore they may need to have lunch around 11.30am so that they can go down at 12.15pm.

Between six and nine months they will also start to roll on to their fronts and prefer to sleep on their tummies. When this happens, it would be advisable to remove the sheets and blankets so as to avoid them getting into a tangle. In the winter months the lightweight sleeping bag will need to be replaced with a warmer one to make up for the loss of blankets.

Feeding

If you have waited until six months to introduce solids it is important that you work through the foods groups fairly quickly. Introduce baby rice after the 11am feed, and then every couple of days introduce a new food, and keep increasing the amounts. Once the babies are taking a reasonable amount of solids at lunch and teatime, you can introduce solids at breakfast. By seven months your baby must be having protein foods at lunchtime, as they will have used up all the iron stored in their body when they were born.

If you were advised to wean your babies earlier than recommended you should be able to introduce protein foods as soon as they reach six months, as their digestive system will be used to digesting different types of foods by this stage.

It is also important that you introduce your babies to a beaker at lunchtime, between the ages of six and seven months, and that you start to use the tier system of feeding at lunchtime. Once your babies are only taking a couple of ounces of milk at lunchtime, replace it with a drink of water or well-diluted juice from a beaker. It is important that this is done once your baby is eating protein at lunchtime. Once the lunchtime milk is dropped they may need to increase the 2.30pm feed. However, if you notice that they are cutting back too much on their last feed, continue to keep this feed smaller.

Between six and seven months, solids should be transferred and changed to a proper tea at 5pm, with only a small drink of water from a beaker, if you have not already done this. They would then have a full milk feed around 6.30pm.

By nine months, if your babies are formula fed they should be drinking all of their water, diluted juice and most of their milk feeds from a beaker.

Routine for twins at nine to twelve months

Feed times	Nap times between 7am and 7pm
7am	9/9.15am–10.00am
11.45am	12.30pm–2.30pm
2.30pm	
5pm	
6.15pm	

Maximum daily sleep 3 hours

7am
- **Babies should be awake, nappy changed and feeding no later than 7am.**
- They should have most of their milk feed, followed by breakfast cereal, mixed with either expressed milk or formula and fruit.
- They can stay awake for between two to two-and-a-half hours.

8am
- They should be encouraged to have a good kick on their play mat for 20-30 minutes.
- Wash and dress both babies, remembering to cream all their creases and dry skin.

9–9.15am
- **Settle both babies, in their cot in the dark with the door shut between 9am and 9.15am.**
- They need a nap of between 30-45 minutes.

9.50am
- Open the curtains and the babies can wake up naturally.

10am
- **Babies must be fully awake now regardless of how long they slept.**
- Encourage them to have a good kick under their play gym or take them on an outing.

11.45am
- They should be given most of their solids before being offered a drink of water or well-diluted juice from a beaker, then alternate between solids and a drink.
- Encourage them to sit in their chairs while you clear away the lunch things.

12.15–12.30pm
- Change their nappies, and settle them in their sleeping bags in the dark with the door shut and no later than 12.30pm.

12.30pm–2.30pm
- **They will need a nap of no longer than two hours from the time they went down.**
- If they slept the full 45 minutes earlier, they may need less sleep at this nap.

2.30pm
- **Babies must be awake and feeding no later than 2.30pm regardless of how long they have slept.**
- Open the curtains, unzip their sleeping bags and allow them to wake up naturally. Change their nappies.
- They need a feed from both breasts or a drink of formula from a beaker.
- **Do not feed them after 3.15pm as it will put them off their next feed.**

4.15pm
- Change the babies' nappies and offer them a drink of cool boiled water or well-diluted juice no later than 4.30pm.

5pm
- They should be given most of their solids before being given a small drink of water or milk from a beaker. It is important that they still have a good milk feed at bedtime, so keep this drink to a minimum.

5.45pm
- Put the babies on their changing mats on the floor without their nappies, so that they can have a good kick while you prepare their bath.

6pm
- They must start their bath no later than 6pm, and be massaged and dressed no later than 6.20pm.

6.20pm
- **Babies should be feeding no later than 6.20pm in a dimly lit room**
- Dim the lights and sit the babies in their chairs for ten minutes or in their cots with a toy or book to look at while you tidy up.

7pm
- **Settle both babies in their cots and in the dark with the door shut, no later than 7pm.**

Changes to be made during the nine-to twelve-months routine

Sleep

The majority of babies cut right back on their daily sleep at this stage. If you notice that your babies are starting to wake earlier in the morning, it is important that you cut back on their total daily sleep.

The first nap to cut back on is the first nap of the day. If they are having 45 minutes, then try cutting it back to 30 minutes. If they have been having only 30 minutes, then cut it back to 10-15 minutes. Some babies may also cut their lunchtime nap right back to one-and-a-half hours, which can lead them to becoming very tired and irritable late afternoon. If this happens to your babies, try cutting out the morning nap altogether to see if it improves their lunchtime sleep. You may have to bring lunchtime forward slightly if they can't make it through to 12.30pm for this nap.

Your babies may also start to pull themselves up in the cot, but get very upset when they can't get themselves back down. If this happens it would be advisable to encourage them to practise laying themselves down when you put them down for their naps. Until they are able to manoeuvre themselves up and down you would need to go in and help them settle back down. It is important that this is done with the least fuss and talking.

Feeding

If your babies start to cut back on their last milk feed, reduce or cut out altogether, the 2.30pm feed. Many babies cut out the 2.30pm feed by one year. As long as they are getting a minimum of 350ml (12oz) of milk a day inclusive of milk used in cereal and cooking, they will be getting enough.

They should be well established on three meals a day, and should also be able to feed themselves some of the time. At nine months formula fed babies should be taking all of their breakfast milk and 2.30pm feed from a beaker.

By the age of one year they should be drinking all their milk and other fluids from a beaker.

Weaning your babies | 8

'Glorious food, great sleep' – Alice

People often remark that I am so lucky to have children with good appetites or who aren't fussy at mealtimes. 'Yes, aren't I just?' I say. What I think, though, is that I have put in months of effort for them to eat as well as they do. I know it's not an Olympic event, but it took serious training from the very first mouthfuls for them to accept a wide variety of flavours and textures, and for them to have respect and appreciation for food. I don't expect a medal, but it has certainly been worth the effort. There are few things in this world more likely to drive you nuts than a small plastic bowl of beautifully prepared organic food being thrown onto a floor that you do not have the energy to clean with kitchen paper that you have run out of.

I don't pretend to be the perfect mother, but I do take pride in knowing that I have done my best. However, the process of introducing solid food to my daughters was just hard work. After the initial excitement of purchasing the high chairs and plastic bowls, and the first flurry of cute photos showing the girls with carrot purée around their mouths, I found the whole feeding process fast became monotonous and time-consuming. The last thing I wanted to buy when I had a rare free hour to hit the shops was a bagful of ice-cube trays. And the last thing I felt like picking up when the clock hit 7pm was a potato peeler. Nonetheless, I spent many hours after my little ones went to bed obsessively preparing their first foods – and I found the peeling and puréeing went much better when accompanied by a bottle of wine.

I have always noticed the relationship between what I eat and how well I feel. Avoiding wheat for four years made me feel fit and energised. Eating pre-prepared food while working late in edit suites at the BBC made me drained and bloated. I was determined to give my girls the very best, and to my mind that meant fresh, organic and home-made. While I had the time and resources, I decided that's what they would eat.

It was about two months into weaning that I first discovered Gina Ford was from north of Watford. Phoebe and Dora, born in May, had been sleeping beautifully through the night from the first week of September until the first week of December. (It's amazing how you don't need to keep a diary to remember these dates. Believe me, when your twins first go from 7pm to 7am, and when they stop three months later, these are days you remember.) I had agreed to do a photo shoot for *Hello!* magazine in aid of TAMBA, the twin and multiple birth charity that had been very supportive during my pregnancy. I hate shoots on the best of days, but when you know you are about a stone above your fighting weight you don't relish the thought of people poring over the final photos. My plan was to look radiant and hold a baby on each hip, thereby concealing a less-than-perfect body and cunningly distracting from my own face with a far more enchanting one on each side. This plan, however, was foiled by a week of sudden unscheduled early wakings. It's impossible to 'do radiant' when your babies have reverted to the sleeping pattern of newborns. We had been so Gina Ford smug about our babies who slept without so much as a squeak from the moment we uncorked the wine to the moment we boiled the kettle in the morning that, apart from suddenly being exhausted, we were completely flummoxed. I drove to the *Hello!* shoot looking pale and drawn. There was no make-up artist on earth who could do radiant on my face. It was at this point that I emailed Gina details of the girls' sleeping patterns and noted down everything they were eating and producing.

Gina rang me at home a little later and I remember putting her on speakerphone so my mother could hear her too. We both got the giggles: here was *the* Gina Ford talking out loud about our little girls in our sitting room. The respect we had for the woman who had given us back our sleep and thus our sanity was further increased when, after short contemplation, she worked out that the girls weren't getting enough protein. Despite clearing their plates, their little growing bodies just needed more. It took about a week to get them back on track. Gina's advice on balancing the food groups and introducing the right foods at the right time was invaluable to me and my family. Problems with two babies can be double the anxiety, so her comments about feeding should be an enormous help to all parents of twins.

~

When to wean

Department of Health (DoH) guidelines published in 2003 were prompted by recommendations from the World Health Organisation. They advise exclusive breast-feeding (no solids or infant formula) for the first six months of a baby's life. The previous DoH advice was to wean between four and six months and not to give solids to any baby before 17 weeks. This is because it takes up to four months for the lining of a baby's gut to develop and for the kidneys to mature enough to cope with the waste products from solid food. If solids are introduced before a baby has the complete set of enzymes required to digest food properly, his digestive system could be damaged. Many experts blame the rapid increase in allergies over the last 20 years on babies being weaned before their digestive system is ready to cope.

During the writing of this book, I have spoken to many dietitians and paediatricians, as well as to hundreds of mothers via my website. It is clear that there is some controversy surrounding the DoH recommendations. Certainly, there are health professionals who feel that it is not weaning between four and six months that threatens a baby's health, but the kinds of food he is given. It is also clear that there are many babies who cannot manage on milk alone for the full six months. If you have any concerns about weaning, I urge you to discuss them with your health visitor or GP and to follow their advice accordingly.

If you follow the weaning plan in this book and introduce the recommended foods in the order suggested, you can be confident that you are not putting your babies at risk of food allergies. It is essential to introduce iron-rich foods at six months as the iron stores with which babies are born become depleted at this age. Iron is essential for healthy red blood cells that transport oxygen around the body. Children who do not take in sufficient amounts of iron are at risk of developing iron-deficiency anaemia, which causes tiredness, irritability and an overall lack of energy and enthusiasm. Up to a quarter of 18-month-old children in the UK show signs of iron deficiency anaemia, so if a breast-fed baby is weaned at six months, it is important that iron-containing foods, such as breakfast cereals, broccoli and lentils, are introduced swiftly. You will need to progress quickly through the food groups to include meat or vegetarian alternatives for their iron content. Babies on formula will have their iron supplemented in the milk.

All babies are individual, so I cannot tell you exactly when yours are ready to wean. However, there are certain signs (listed overleaf) that indicate the time has come. Watch closely for these, remembering that your twins might not both be ready at the same time, and be aware that they might come sooner than the current DoH recommendations. If your babies are under six months of age and showing all the signs below, it is vital you discuss things with your health visitor or GP and decide with them whether to wean early or not.

Ready to wean?

Your babies could be ready to wean if they meet the following criteria:

- They have been taking a full feed four or five times a day from both breasts, or a 240ml (8oz) bottle of formula, and have been going happily for four hours between feeds, but now get irritable and chew their hands long before the next feed is due.
- They have been taking a full feed from both breasts or a 240ml (8oz) formula-feed and scream for more the minute the feed finishes.
- They usually sleep well at night and nap times, but are starting to wake up earlier and earlier.
- They are chewing their hands excessively, displaying eye-to-hand co-ordination and trying to put things into their mouth.

If one or both of your babies is at least four months old, has doubled his birth weight and is consistently displaying most of the signs above, he is probably ready to begin weaning. If the baby is under six months, you should tell your health visitor or GP and decide how to proceed. If you decide to wait until the babies are six months before you introduce solids, it is important that their increased hunger is met by introducing further milk feeds. Babies who have been sleeping through the night with only a small feed at 10/11pm need to have this feed increased. And if they go through a further growth spurt before they reach six months, it may be that you need to introduce a further feed in the middle of the night. It is very important to understand that as your babies grow, so will their appetites. If you wish to continue exclusively breast-feeding until six months, it is unreasonable to expect the babies to manage on only four milk feeds a day.

Breast-fed babies

With babies who are being fully breast-fed, it is more difficult to tell how much milk they are receiving. If they are over four months and showing most of the ready-to-wean signs, you will need to talk in depth to your health visitor or GP about the choices on offer.

If they are under four months and not gaining enough weight each week, it is possible that your milk supply is getting very low in the evening, especially with two to feed. All that may be needed is extra milk, not solids, so I suggest you try topping up the babies with 60ml (2oz) of expressed milk or formula after the 10pm feed. If this does not work, or if they are waking up more than once in the night, I would replace the 10pm feed altogether with full bottle-feeds for each of them. Encourage your partner to do this feed so that you can get to bed early, after expressing whatever milk you have at 9pm to avoid your supply dropping any further. Mothers in this situation often find that when they express, they are producing only 90–120ml (3–4oz), which is much less than their baby may need at this feed. The milk expressed can, if necessary, be given at some other feed during the day, thus avoiding further complementary bottle-feeding.

This plan usually satisfies a baby's hunger and improves his weight gain. **Remember: you should never wean a baby before 17 weeks of age, and doing so sooner than six months should be done only on medical advice.**

Feeding two babies

I have looked after 16 sets of twins. Whenever possible, for hygiene reasons and to avoid cross-infection, I always tried to keep separate bowls and spoons for each baby. If one has a cold coming or any other infection, keeping them to their own things helps avoid both becoming ill. Two sick babies is no fun at all. Of course, I am realistic as well. With two babies screaming for food at the same time, you can find yourself literally shovelling it into each of them as fast as you can, and your well-intentioned hygiene standards fly out of the window. Just do your best in this respect, but be especially careful if you know one or the other is unwell.

For the first week or two of weaning, I often found that the babies missed the physical closeness involved in a breast-feed or bottle-feed. Putting them straight into high chairs for their first tastes of food can be alarming if they are suddenly parted from you. What I found easiest was to put the babies side by side together on the floor in their bouncy chairs and then sit in between them on a sofa to keep that sense of closeness. Feeding them downwards also means that you don't have to stretch far to reach them. Once they are enjoying new foods and have become used to the spoon, you can put them in high chairs at the table.

Your babies will take differently to different foods, and you will quickly learn each child's preferences. They are individuals who will develop their own tastes, but you are not a five-star hotel and shouldn't start accommodating every whim at the early stages. It might not feel unreasonable when they are having just one solid meal a day at the beginning, but once they are established on three meals a day by the end of seven months, you won't want to be preparing different foods every time you sit them at the table. At each meal choose one of the food groups that they both like and encourage them to eat it. If one prefers carrot to broccoli, for example, you can have an extra cube of their favourite ready for each of them.

Foods to be avoided

During the first two years of your babies' lives, certain foods are best used sparingly, or avoided altogether, as they may be harmful to your babies' health. The two worst culprits in this regard are sugar and salt.

Sugar

During the first year of weaning, it is best to avoid adding sugar to any of your babies' food, as it may lead to them developing a taste for sweet things. A baby's appetite for savoury foods can be seriously affected if he is allowed lots of food containing sugar or sugar substitutes. Unfortunately, when buying ready-made foods, these ingredients can be hard to avoid. A survey by the Consumer's Association magazine *Which?* tested 420 baby products and reported that 40 per cent contained sugar or fruit juice or both. When choosing baby cereals or ready-made foods, check the labels carefully; sugar may be listed as dextrose, fructose, glucose or sucrose. Watch out too for syrup and concentrated fruit juice, which are also sometimes used as sweeteners.

Too much sugar in the diet may not only make your babies refuse savoury food, but can lead to serious problems such as tooth decay and obesity. Sugar converts very quickly into energy, so babies and children who have too much may also become hyperactive. Products such as baked beans, spaghetti hoops, cornflakes, fish fingers, jam, tomato ketchup, tinned soups and some yoghurts are just a few of the everyday foods that contain hidden sugars, so take care when your babies reach toddlerhood that they do not eat these foods in excess. It is also important to check the labels of fruit juices and squashes.

Salt

Children under two years of age should not have salt added to their food: they get all the salt they need from natural sources, such as vegetables. Adding salt to a young baby's food can be very dangerous as it can put a strain on his immature kidneys. Research also shows that adding salt might make children more prone to heart disease later. When your babies reach the important stage of joining in with family meals, it is important that you do not add salt to the food during cooking. Remove your babies' portions, then add salt for the rest of the family, if necessary.

Like sugar, salt is also present at high levels in many processed foods and ready-made meals. It is important to check the labels on these items carefully before giving them to your toddler.

Preparing and cooking food for your babies

Making your own baby food often works out cheaper than buying ready-made, but even more important is that it will be of greater nutritional benefit to your babies. Doing it yourself needn't be a constant chore or dominate your days if you make up large quantities at a time and store mini-meals away in the freezer. Keep sterilised feeding equipment, ice-cube trays and freezer-proof containers at the ready, and follow the general instructions below.

- When preparing food, always ensure that work surfaces and chopping boards are spotless and have been wiped down with an anti-bacterial cleaner. Use kitchen paper for cleaning and drying surfaces, as it is more hygienic than kitchen cloths and towels, which may carry bacteria.
- All fresh fruit and vegetables should be carefully peeled, and the core, pips and any blemishes removed. They should then be rinsed thoroughly with filtered water.
- If you are advised to wean your babies early, remember that all fruit and vegetables must be cooked until your babies are six months old. This can be done by steaming or boiling them in filtered water. Do not add salt, sugar or honey.
- During the initial stages of weaning, all food must be cooked until soft enough to purée to a very smooth consistency similar to that of yoghurt. A small amount of the cooking water can be added to achieve this.
- If using a food processor, check carefully for lumps by using a spoon and pouring the mixture into another bowl. When satisfied that the texture is right, transfer to ice-cube trays or small containers for storage in the freezer.

Sterilising equipment

All feeding equipment should be sterilised for the first six months, and bottles and teats should be sterilised for as long as they are used. Sterilise ice-cube trays or freezer containers by boiling them in a large saucepan of water for five minutes. Use a steam steriliser, if you have one, for small items such as spoons or serving bowls, and follow the timings recommended in the manufacturer's handbook. Wash cooking utensils as usual in a dishwasher, or rinse hand-washed items with boiling water from the kettle.

Packing food for the freezer

For reasons of hygiene and food safety, take the following precautions when storing home-made food for your babies.

- Check the temperature of your freezer on a freezer thermometer (available from cookware shops and department stores). It should read minus 18°C.
- Make sure cooked, puréed food is covered as quickly as possible, and transfer it to the freezer as soon as it's cold.
- Never put warm food into a refrigerator or freezer.
- When ice-cube trays of puréed food are cold, open-freeze them until solid, then pop the cubes out of the tray and into a sterilised plastic box. Non-sterilised items, such as plastic bags, can be used from six months. Seal well and return to the freezer.
- Label items clearly, adding the date.
- Use foods within six months.
- Never refreeze cooked food. However, items that were originally frozen raw then defrosted and cooked, such as chicken portions that have been made into a casserole, can be safely refrozen.

Defrosting tips

- Defrost frozen food in the fridge overnight, or leave at room temperature if you forget, transferring it to the fridge as soon as it has defrosted. Make sure it is covered at all times, and stand it on a plate to catch the drips.

- Never speed up defrosting by putting food into warm or hot water.
- Always use defrosted foods within 24 hours.

Reheating tips

- Food should be heated thoroughly to ensure that any bacteria are killed. If using jars, always transfer the contents to a dish; never serve straight from the jar. Any food left over should be discarded, never reheated and used again.
- When batch cooking, take out a portion of food for your babies to use now and freeze the rest. Don't be tempted to reheat the entire mixture and then freeze what is left.
- If your babies have eaten only a tiny amount of what you have heated up, it can be tempting to reheat and serve it later. Please don't. Babies are much more susceptible than adults to food poisoning, so get into the habit of throwing leftovers away immediately.
- Reheat foods only once.

Early weaning

If you have been advised that your babies are ready for weaning before the recommended age of six months, it is important to remember that milk is still the most important food for them because it provides the right balance of vitamins and minerals. Solids given before six months are classed as 'first tastes' and 'fillers', which should be increased very slowly over several weeks, gradually preparing your babies for three solid meals a day. By offering the milk first, you will ensure that their daily milk intake does not decrease too rapidly before they reach six months.

Studies into weaning by the University of Surrey revealed that babies fed diets with a high fruit content may be more prone to diarrhoea, which leads to slow growth. They advise that baby rice is the best first weaning food as fruit may not be so well tolerated by the underdeveloped gut of some babies.

Remember that as soon as your babies have teeth and have begun on any type of solid food, they will need their teeth cleaning twice a day, preferably after each meal.

How to begin weaning

- Introduce solids after the 11am feed. Prepare in advance everything you need for giving the solids: two baby chairs, two bibs, two spoons, two bowls and two clean damp cloths.
- Start by offering each baby a teaspoonful of pure organic rice mixed to a very smooth consistency with expressed milk, formula or cool, freshly boiled filtered water.
- Make sure the rice is cool enough before feeding it to your babies. Use a shallow plastic spoon for each of them, never a metal one, which can be too sharp or get too hot.
- Some babies need help in learning how to feed from a spoon. Place the spoon just inside the mouth and bring it up and out against the roof of the mouth so that the upper gums take the food off.
- Once your babies are established on baby rice at 11am and are tolerating it, give the rice after the 6pm feed instead. When they finish the one teaspoonful and show signs of looking for more food, the amount of solids can be increased, provided they continue to take the required amount of milk at 6pm.
- Once your babies are happily taking 1–2 teaspoonfuls of baby rice mixed with milk or water after the 6pm feed, a small amount of pear purée can be introduced after the 11am feed. With babies under six months, this usually happens between the fourth and sixth day, and with babies over six months, it will probably happen between the second and fourth day.
- Be guided by each of your babies as to when to increase the amounts. They will turn their heads away and get fussy when they have had enough.

- If the babies tolerate the pear purée, transfer it to the 6pm feed. Mixing the purée with baby rice in the evening will make it more palatable and prevent your babies from getting constipated.
- Small amounts of various organic vegetables and fruit can now be introduced after the 11am feed. To prevent your babies from developing a sweet tooth, try to give more vegetables than fruit. At this stage, avoid the stronger-tasting ones, such as spinach or broccoli, and concentrate instead on root vegetables, such as carrot, sweet potato and swede. These contain natural sugars, so they will taste sweeter and blander, and may prove more palatable to your babies.
- With babies under six months it is important to introduce new foods in small amounts every 3–4 days. Increasing 1–2 teaspoonfuls a week between the two meals is a good guideline. Babies over six months will probably need their meals increased by larger amounts every couple of days, and as long as you stick to the foods listed in first-stage weaning (see page 192), you can introduce new foods closer together. Keeping a food diary will help you to see how your babies react to each new food.
- Always be very positive and smile when offering new foods. If your babies spit a food out, it may not mean they dislike it. Remember this is all very new to them, and different foods will get different reactions from each of them. If they positively refuse a food, however, leave it and try again in a week's time.
- Always offer milk first, as this is still the most important food in nutritional terms at this stage. While appetites do vary, in my experience the majority of babies will be drinking 840–900ml (28–30oz) of formula a day, or 4–5 full breast-feeds. Provided your babies are happy and thriving, the minimum recommended amount of milk required at this age is 600ml (20oz) a day.

For more comprehensive advice on weaning, including daily plans and recipes you can prepare for your babies, see *The*

Contented Little Baby Book of Weaning. There are also many more easy-to-prepare recipes for babies and toddlers in *The Gina Ford Baby and Toddler Cook Book.*

First-stage weaning: six to seven months

If your babies started weaning before six months, they will probably have tasted baby rice, plus a variety of different vegetables and fruits. Follow my guidelines in Early weaning (see page 188) for when to start baby rice and when to introduce fruit and vegetables. Once you have started weaning, it is important to keep introducing a variety of the different fruits and vegetables listed on the following page in the first-stage weaning foods. All fruit and vegetables should still be steamed or cooked in filtered water until soft, then puréed. Mix to the desired consistency with some of the cooking water; unsalted chicken stock may be used with different vegetables.

At this stage you should avoid introducing dairy products, wheat, eggs, nuts and citrus fruit as they are the foods most likely to trigger allergies. Honey should *not* be introduced before one year. Do not introduce protein (meat, chicken and fish) until the babies are capable of digesting reasonable amounts of other solids. Some nutritionists believe that protein can put a strain on the young baby's kidneys and digestive tract. I agree with this, as all too often I have seen feeding problems occur because meat, poultry or fish have been introduced too early. Once you have worked through the first foods, you can introduce protein. In the meantime, your first sources of iron can be found in lentils, broccoli and iron-rich breakfast cereals.

When beginning weaning at the age of six months, you will need to progress quickly through the first-stage foods so that the iron-rich meat and vegetarian products can be introduced and eaten regularly. As a rough guideline, increase the baby rice at teatime by one teaspoonful every couple of days, and increase the savoury at lunchtime by one cube (one tablespoon) every couple of days. It is also essential to gradually reduce your babies' milk intake to four feeds a day once solids are established.

Between six and seven months, depending on when you began weaning, your babies should be having 2–3 servings of carbohydrates daily in the form of cereal, wholemeal bread, pasta or potatoes. They should each also have three servings of vegetables or fruit each day, and one serving of animal or vegetable protein.

Foods to introduce

Pure organic baby rice, pear, apple, carrot, sweet potato, potatoes, green beans, courgettes and swede are ideal first weaning foods. Once your babies are happily taking these things, you can introduce parsnips, mango, peaches, broccoli, avocados, barley, peas and cauliflower.

Protein, in the form of meat, poultry, fish and lentils, should be introduced by the seventh month, once solids are established. Check that all bones are removed and trim off the fat and the skin. Some babies find the flavour of protein cooked on its own too strong, so try cooking chicken or meat in a casserole with familiar root vegetables, and cook fish in a milk sauce until your babies become accustomed to the different textures and tastes. Both can be pulsed in a food processor.

Start introducing protein at lunchtime, as it is harder to digest than carbohydrate and will be digested by bedtime.

Breakfast

A baby is ready to start having breakfast once he shows signs of hunger long before his 11am feed. This usually happens between the ages of six and seven months. All cereal should be wheat-free and gluten-free until the age of six months. I find that organic oatmeal cereal with a small amount of puréed fruit is a favourite with most babies.

You should still give your babies most of their milk feed first. After a couple of weeks give about two-thirds of the milk first, then the cereal, finishing up with the remainder of the milk feed. If your babies reach seven months and show no sign of wanting breakfast, it would be wise to reduce their milk feeds very slightly and offer a small amount of solids.

Lunch

Start by replacing some of the vegetable cubes you introduced at the 11am feed with two cubes of the more simple chicken, fish, meat or pulse recipes (see *The Contented Little Baby Book of Weaning* and *The Gina Ford Baby and Toddler Cook Book*). Introduce new foods very slowly during the early stage. A new food every three days is about right, and you should take careful note of what each baby eats and any reactions they might have. Increase the amount by one or two cubes a day until your babies' meals consist totally of one of the protein recipes.

Introducing a beaker

Once protein is introduced at lunchtime, the milk feed must be replaced by a drink of water or well-diluted juice from a beaker. Most babies of six months are capable of sipping and swallowing, and this should be encouraged by being consistent and always offering the lunchtime drink from a beaker. Do not worry if your babies drink only a small amount at this meal; you will probably find that they make up for it at their 2.30pm milk feed.

Tea

At some point during the sixth month, the cereal and fruit given at the 6pm feed can be replaced by a proper (vegetarian) tea at 5pm. If you always make sure that your babies have a well-balanced breakfast and lunch, you can be relaxed about this meal. Once breakfast and lunch are established, you can sit the babies down at 5pm and offer them a small tea. Some babies can get very fractious around this time of the day, so offer foods that are quick and easy to prepare: thick vegetable soups and vegetable bakes that have been made and frozen in advance are always a good standby. Pasta or baked potatoes served with vegetables and sauces are also nutritious and easy. A very hungry baby can also be offered a milk pudding or yoghurt.

Daily requirements

By six months, babies who started weaning early will probably be established on two solid meals a day and heading towards a third. Getting the balance of solids right is vital so that they continue to get the right amount of milk. Although they will have cut down on the 11am breast-feed or bottle-feed as their intake of solids increases, they still need a minimum of 600ml (20oz) of milk a day, divided between 3–4 feeds. Babies who started weaning at six months will probably still be having five or six milk feeds a day, which you need to reduce gradually.

Some babies who are still drinking large amounts of milk at six months may be resistant to the introduction of solids. If you find that either of your babies is fussy about taking solids, you should offer them only half their milk at the 11am feed to encourage interest in the solid food. The aim is to have the babies on two meals a day within a couple of weeks of beginning solids. By the time they reach seven months, regardless of when they began weaning, all babies should be well established on two meals a day, progressing to three meals that consist of a wide variety of foods from the different food groups.

At the end of six months a typical day's menu might look something like this:

7/7.30am	**Breakfast**
	Breast-feed or 210–240ml (7–8oz) of formula milk
	2–4 teaspoons of oat cereal mixed with expressed milk or formula, plus 1 or 2 cubes of fruit purée

11.30am	**Lunch**
	Small breast-feed or 90–120ml (3–4oz) of formula milk
	4–6 cubes of vegetable purée, including small amounts of animal or vegetarian protein
2/2.30pm	**Afternoon**
	Breast-feed or 150–210ml (5–7oz) of formula milk
5pm	**Tea**
	5–6 teaspoons of baby rice mixed with expressed or formula milk, plus 2 cubes of fruit purée, heading towards a proper savoury tea with a drink of water, milk or well-diluted juice from a beaker
6.30pm	Breast-feed or 180–240ml (6–8oz) of formula milk
10pm	Feed optional

Once a baby is established on three good solid meals a day plus three or four full milk feeds, he should manage to go nearer to 12 hours at night without a feed. If your babies are not cutting down on their 10pm feed once solids are introduced, it may be that they are not getting the right quantities of solids for their age or weight, or a too-small feed at 6.30pm. Keep a diary of all the food and milk consumed by each twin over a period of four days to help pinpoint why they are not cutting that last feed.

By the end of six months your babies will probably be ready to sit in high chairs for their meals. Always ensure that they are properly strapped in and never left unattended.

Second-stage weaning: seven to nine months

During the second stage of weaning, the amount of milk your babies drink will gradually reduce as their intake of solids increases. However, it is important that they still receive a minimum of 500–600ml (17–20oz) a day of breast or formula milk. This is usually divided between three milk feeds and milk used in food and cooking as sauces are introduced. At this stage of weaning you should be aiming at establishing three good solid meals a day so that by the time your babies reach nine months of age they are getting most of their nourishment from solids. During this time it is important to keep introducing a wide variety of foods from the different food groups (carbohydrate, protein, dairy, fruit and vegetables) so that your babies' nutritional needs are met.

Most babies are ready to accept stronger-tasting foods at this age. They also take pleasure from different textures, colours and presentation. Foods should be individually mashed or pulsed in a food processor as babies do not like everything mixed up. Fruit can be grated or mashed rather than cooked. It is also around this age that your babies will begin to put food in their mouths. Raw soft fruit, lightly cooked vegetables and toast can be used as finger foods. They will be sucked and squeezed more than eaten at this stage, but allowing them the opportunity to feed themselves encourages good feeding habits later on. Once your babies are having finger foods, always wash their hands before a meal and never leave them alone while they are eating.

Between eight and nine months your babies may show signs of wanting to use their spoons. To encourage this, provide two spoons for each of them. Load one for each of them to try feeding themselves. You use the others for actually getting the food in. You can help their co-ordination by holding their wrists gently and guiding the spoons into their mouths.

Foods to introduce

Dairy products, pasta and wheat can also be introduced at this stage. Full-fat cow's milk can be used in cooking, but should not be given as a drink until one year. Small amounts of unsalted butter can also be used in cooking. Egg yolks can be introduced, but must be hard-boiled. Cheese should be full fat, pasteurised and grated, and preferably organic. Olive oil can be used when cooking casseroles.

Tinned fish, such as tuna, may also be included, but choose those in vegetable oil, as those in brine have a higher salt content. A greater variety of vegetables can now be introduced, including coloured peppers, Brussels sprouts, pumpkin, cabbage and spinach. Tomatoes and well-diluted, unsweetened fruit juices can be included if there is no history of allergies. All these foods should be introduced gradually and careful notes made of any reactions.

Once your babies are used to taking food from a spoon, vegetables can be mashed rather than puréed. When they are happy taking mashed food you can start to introduce small amounts of finger food. Vegetables should be cooked until soft, then offered in cube-sized pieces, or steamed and mixed to the right consistency. Once your babies are managing softly cooked pieces of vegetables and soft pieces of raw fruit, you can try them with toast or a low-sugar rusk. By nine months, if your babies have several teeth, they should be able to manage some chopped raw vegetables. Dried fruit can also be given now, but it should be washed first and soaked overnight.

Breakfast

Sugar-free, unrefined wheat cereals can now be introduced; choose ones fortified with iron and B vitamins. You may want to delay introducing these if you have a family history of allergies; check with your health visitor or GP, or a dietitian. Try adding a little mashed or grated fruit if your babies refuse it. Try to alternate between oat-based and wheat-based cereals, even if your babies show a preference for one over the other. You can encourage your babies with finger foods by offering them a little buttered toast at this stage. Once they are finger-feeding, you can offer a selection of fruits and yoghurts along with lightly buttered toast.

Most babies are still desperate for their milk first thing in the morning, so still allow them two-thirds of it first. Once they are nearly nine months of age, they will probably show signs of not being hungry for milk, and this is the time to try offering breakfast milk from a beaker.

Lunch

If your babies are eating a proper breakfast, you will be able to push lunch to somewhere between 11.45am and 12 noon. However, should they be eating only a small amount of breakfast, lunch will need to come slightly earlier. Likewise, babies who are having only a very short nap in the morning may also need to have lunch earlier. It's important to remember that overtired, over-hungry babies will not feed as well, so take your timing of lunch from them.

During this stage of weaning you will have established protein at lunchtime. Whenever possible, try to buy organic chicken and meat that is free from additives and growth stimulators. Pork, bacon and processed hams should not be introduced as they have a high salt content. You should still continue to cook without additional salt or sugar, although a small amount of herbs can be introduced at around nine months of age.

Once protein is well established, your babies' milk feed should be replaced at lunchtime by a drink of cool, boiled water or well-diluted juice from a beaker. You might find that they drink only a small amount from the beaker and look for an increase of milk at the 2.30pm feed, or an increase of cool, boiled water later in the day.

If you are introducing your babies to a vegetarian diet, it is important to seek expert advice on getting the right balance of amino acids. Vegetables are incomplete sources of amino acids when cooked separately, and need to be combined correctly to provide your babies with a complete source of protein.

If your babies are still hungry after their main meal, offer a piece of cheese, a breadstick, chopped fruit or yoghurt.

Tea

Once your babies are finger-feeding, tea can be a selection of mini sandwiches, or a baked potato or pasta served with vegetables and a sauce. Some babies get very tired and fussy by teatime. If your babies do not eat much, try offering some rice pudding or a yoghurt. A small drink of water from a beaker can be offered after the tea. Do not allow too large a drink at this time as it will put them off their last milk feed. Their bedtime milk feed is still important at this stage. If they start cutting back too much on this feed, check that you are not overfeeding them on solids or giving them too much to drink.

Daily requirements

At this second stage of weaning it is important that you work towards establishing your babies on three proper meals a day. These should include three servings of carbohydrates, such as cereals, bread and pasta, plus at least three servings of vegetables and fruit, and one serving of puréed meat, fish or pulses. By six months a baby has used up all the stores of iron he was born with. As their requirements between six and 12 months are particularly high, it is important that their diet provides the right amount of iron. To help iron absorption from cereals and meat, always serve with fruit or vegetables, and avoid giving milk to drink with protein as it reduces the iron content by 50 per cent.

The babies still need 500–600ml (17–20oz) of breast or formula milk a day inclusive of milk used for mixing food. If your babies start to reject their milk, try giving them more cheese, milk sauces and yoghurt. By the end of nine months try to encourage your babies to drink all their breakfast milk from a beaker. Apart from their bedtime milk, all other milk feeds and drinks should ideally be from a beaker.

A very hungry baby who is taking three full milk feeds a day plus three solid meals may need a small drink and a piece of fruit mid-morning.

A typical day for twins of 8–9 months would look like this:

7/7.30am	**Breakfast**
	Breast-feed or 210–240ml (7–8oz) of formula milk in a beaker
	Mixed mashed fruit and yoghurt, or wheat/oat cereal with milk and mashed fruit
11.45am/12 noon	**Lunch**
	Chicken risotto with chopped Brussels sprouts, cauliflower florets and diced potato, or tuna pasta
	Drink of water or well-diluted juice from a beaker
2/2.30pm	**Afternoon**
	Breast-feed or 150–180ml (5–6oz) of formula milk
5pm	**Tea**
	Vegetable broth with mini sandwiches, or creamy pasta with spring vegetables
	Drink of water or well-diluted juice from a beaker
6.30pm	Breast-feed or 180–240ml (6–8oz) of formula milk

Third-stage weaning: nine to twelve months

Between nine and 12 months your babies should be eating and enjoying all types of food, apart from those with a high fat, salt or sugar content. Peanuts and honey should also still be avoided. It is very important that your babies learn to chew properly at this stage. Food should be chopped or diced, although meat still needs to be pulsed or very finely chopped. By the end of their first year, they should be able to manage chopped meat.

This is also a good time to introduce raw vegetables and salads. Try to include some finger foods at every meal, and if your babies show an interest in holding their own spoons, do not discourage these attempts. It is important that they enjoy their meals, even if a certain amount of food lands on the floor.

Breakfast

Encourage your babies to take at least some of their breakfast milk feed from a beaker. By the end of the first year they should be drinking all of their breakfast milk from a beaker. Aim to get each of them to take 210ml (7oz) of milk each at this meal, divided between a drink and their breakfast cereal. Scrambled egg can be offered once or twice a week as a change.

Lunch

Lunch should consist of a wide selection of lightly steamed, chopped vegetables with a daily serving of meat or meat alternative. Babies of this age are very active and can become quite tired and irritable by 5pm. By ensuring a well-balanced lunch, you will not need to worry if tea is more relaxed. By the end of the first year your babies' lunch can be integrated with the family lunch. Prepare the meal without salt, sugar or spices and reserve a portion for the babies, then add the desired flavourings for the rest of the family.

Try to ensure that their meals are attractively presented, with a variety of different coloured vegetables and fruit. Do not overload their plates; serve up a small amount, and when they finish that, replenish their plates. This also helps to avoid the game of throwing food on the floor, which often occurs at this stage. If your babies do start to play up with their main course, refusing to eat and throwing food on the floor, quietly and firmly say 'No' and remove the plate. Do not offer them a biscuit or fromage frais half an hour later, as a pattern will soon emerge where they will refuse lunch, knowing that they will get something sweet if they play up enough. A piece of fruit can be offered mid-afternoon to see them through to tea, at which time they will probably eat very well.

A drink of well-diluted, pure, unsweetened orange juice in a beaker will help the absorption of iron at this meal, but make sure they have most of their meal before you allow them to finish the drink.

Tea

Many babies cut out their 2.30pm milk during this stage. If you are worried that your twins' daily milk intake is too low, try giving them things at teatime such as pasta and vegetables with a milk sauce, baked potatoes with grated cheese, cheesy vegetable bake or mini quiches. Tea is usually the meal when I give small helpings of milk pudding or fromage frais, which are also alternatives if milk is being rejected. Regularly try to include some finger foods at teatime.

The bedtime bottle should be discouraged after one year, so during this stage get your babies gradually used to less milk at bedtime. This can be done by offering them a small drink of milk with their teatime meal, then a drink of 150–180ml (5–6oz) of milk from a beaker at bedtime.

Daily requirements

By one year it is important that large volumes of milk are discouraged; no more than 600ml (20oz), inclusive of milk used in food, should be allowed. After one year your babies each need a minimum of 350ml (12oz) a day. This is usually divided between two or three drinks and includes milk used in cooking or on cereals.

Full-fat, pasteurised cow's milk can be given to drink after one year. If your babies refuse cow's milk, try gradually diluting their formula with it until they are happy to take full cow's milk. If possible, try to give your babies organic cow's milk as it comes from cows fed exclusively on grass, unlike unorganic milk, which comes from cows fed on a diet of animal offal. The cows have difficulty in digesting the meat, so a proportion is turned into mucus in the digestive system. This is excreted via the udders, resulting in milk with a mucus content as high as 30 per cent compared to the 5 per cent found in organic milk.

Encourage three well-balanced meals a day and avoid snacks of biscuits, cakes and crisps. Every day aim for each baby to have 3–4 servings of carbohydrate, 3–4 servings of fruit and vegetables, and one portion of animal protein or two of vegetable protein.

Your questions answered

Q How will I know when my babies are ready to be weaned?

A • If your babies have been sleeping through, but then start to wake up in the night or very early in the morning and will not settle back to sleep.

• A bottle-fed baby taking in excess of 960–1140ml (32–38oz) a day, draining a 240ml (8oz) bottle at each feed and looking for another feed long before it is due.

• A breast-fed baby would start to look for a feed every 2–3 hours.

• Both breast-fed and bottle-fed babies would start to chew on their hands a lot and be very irritable in between feeds.

• If unsure, always talk to your health visitor or paediatrician, and especially if your babies are less than six months old.

Q What would happen if I weaned my babies before they are ready?

A • Their digestive system could be harmed if they have not developed the complete set of enzymes required to digest solids.

• Introducing solids before they are ready could lead to allergies.

• Studies from several different countries show that persistent coughs and wheezing are more common in babies who were weaned before 17 weeks.

Q At what milk feed should I introduce solids?

A • I usually start at the 11am feed as this will gradually be pushed to 12 noon, becoming a proper lunch once solids become established.

• Milk is still the most important source of food. By giving solids after this feed you can be sure that your babies will have at least half their daily milk intake before noon.

• Solids offered at the 2.30pm feed seem to put babies off the very important 6pm feed.

• If a very hungry baby has no adverse reaction to the baby rice within three days, I would transfer the rice to after the 6pm feed.

Q Which is the best food to introduce?

A • I find pure organic baby rice is the food that satisfies most babies' hunger the best. If this is tolerated, I would then introduce some organic puréed pear.

• Once these two foods are established, it is best to concentrate on introducing a variety of vegetables from the first stage of weaning (see page 192).

• In a survey carried out by the University of Surrey it was found that babies weaned on fruit were less likely to thrive than babies weaned on baby rice. They advise that all babies should start weaning on baby rice.

Q How will I know how much solid food to give my babies?

A • For the first six months milk is still the most important part of your babies' diet. It will provide them with the right balance of vitamins and minerals, so they will each need a minimum of 600ml (20oz) a day. During the first month of weaning, if you always offer the milk feed before the solids, you can be sure they will take exactly the amount of solids they need. This avoids them replacing their milk too quickly with solids.

• Between five and six months you can start the 11am feed by giving half the milk feed first, then some solids, followed by more milk. This will encourage your babies to cut back slightly on their milk feed and increase their solids, preparing them for a feeding pattern of three meals a day at six months.

- With breast-fed babies, a feed from one breast can be classed as half a milk feed.

Q At what age should I start to reduce the amount of milk they drink?

A • Up to the age of six months your babies still need a minimum of 600ml (20oz) of milk a day each. From five months more milk will be used to mix their rice, cereals and solids, so the actual amount they drink reduces slightly, but their daily intake should remain much the same.

- As they increase their solids, the feeds they should cut back on are the 11am and 2.30pm.

- Your babies should be established on the tier system at lunchtime by six months.

- Once your babies are established on three meals a day, introduce the tier-system breakfast (see pages 170–1).

Q My son Matthew is almost nine months old and has been refusing cereal after being giving most of his milk. I have offered him toast, of which he eats some. He is now refusing to eat anything that I offer to him on a spoon, and this is happening at teatime as well. He has a fifth tooth coming through, but he goes to nursery one day a week and always feeds well there. His twin brother is a good feeder and consistently eats a good amount.

A • Now that your twins are almost nine months old they will probably not be so hungry for their milk first thing in the morning. Begin to offer it in a beaker along with their cereal. If Matthew's lack of interest continues, try a different cereal as some babies do get bored with the same one or two cereals offered daily.

- At mealtimes offer him a spoon to hold and encourage him to have a go at feeding himself. Begin with easy things, such as mashed potato, which will stay on his spoon quite well. It may take him a while to get the hang of feeding himself, but it will keep him absorbed and he will not notice that you are also feeding him.

- Continue to offer him finger foods. Handling these is another skill that needs to be learnt. Try with steamed vegetable batons and offer them with a dip. Show him how to dunk his vegetables. Use pieces of bread roll dipped in a casserole dish. Offer this to him while you are feeding him from his bowl. Having something to hold in their hands and keep them occupied often helps with babies of this age who are on a food strike. When you are serving a thick vegetable soup, give him a finger of toast or mini sandwich to dip into it.

- Begin to push lunch on to 11.45/12 noon. Now the twins are older they will be able to wait longer, unless they had a very short morning nap and are too tired to eat lunch properly.

Q At what age do I start to cut out milk feeds altogether?

A • Assuming your babies were on five milk feeds when they started to wean, once three solid meals are well established, they should automatically cut back on their 10pm feed, and cut it out altogether somewhere between four and five months.

- The next feed to cut out would be the 11am feed. Once your babies are having chicken or fish for lunch, the milk feed should be replaced with a drink of water or well-diluted juice from a beaker.

- The 2.30pm feed often increases for a few months, then somewhere between nine and 12 months they will lose interest in this feed, at which time it can be dropped.

Q At what age should I introduce a beaker and at which feeds?

A • Between the ages of six and seven months is the best time to introduce a beaker.

- When you have replaced the lunchtime milk feed with

water or well-diluted juice, try giving it from a beaker or a bottle with a hard spout.

- Try offering it halfway through the meal and after every few spoonfuls of food.
- It is important to persevere. Experiment with different types of beaker until you find one with which your babies are happy.
- Once they are each taking 60–90ml (2–3oz) from a beaker, gradually introduce it at other feeds.
- The Department of Health report recommends that bottle-feeding is discouraged after one year, as it will decrease the appetite for other foods.

Q When can I introduce cow's milk?

A • I usually introduce a small amount of organic cow's milk in cooking from six months.
- Cow's milk should not be given as a drink until your babies are at least one year old.
- It should always be full-fat pasteurised milk, preferably organic.
- If your babies refuse cow's milk, try mixing it half and half with formula. Once they are happy taking that, gradually increase the cow's milk until they are happy with all cow's milk.

Q My twins are 11 months. They both had quite severe reflux in the early days, so gained weight slowly. They now receive medication and are much improved, but they have never really enjoyed milk. One twin (Tom) absolutely refuses his 6.30pm bottle. He now screams and turns his head away just at the sight of it. He has three meals a day and is taking solids well. He drinks water well with meals. In the morning he takes his milk happily. Since bringing tea forward to 5pm about two months ago, he has become upset and starts crying as soon as he is out of the bath. His twin, who is the same weight and in the same routine, accepts his milk.

A • As Tom's refusal coincided with his tea being moved to 5pm, it would be worth considering that he is not really hungry for it. He is also probably beginning to use much more energy at this time by crawling and pulling himself up, so he is very tired by the time he has had a bath.

• In order to increase his small milk intake, move tea to 4.45pm and offer him a small drink of milk from a beaker halfway through the meal. If he accepts this, he will have already increased his intake by 90–120ml (3–4oz). Include plenty of cheesy pasta bakes, pieces of quiche and jacket potatoes with cheese. Give him some yoghurt or a small fromage frais with his fruit. All this will add to his daily total of dairy products.

• To stop him getting too tired, make bathtime 15 minutes earlier and see if he still reacts in the same way afterwards. Offer him a smaller bottle if he has taken some milk at teatime. Keeping a watchful eye on his milk intake will help him to continue gaining weight, even though he has taken to solids well.

Q At what age can I stop puréeing their food?
A • Once they have taken well to puréed food (hopefully by the end of the sixth month), you can start to mash the vegetables and fruit by hand: there should be no lumps, but it will not be as smooth as the puréed food.

• Between six and nine months gradually mash the food less and less until the babies will take food with lumps in it.

• Chicken and meat should still be pulsed until your babies are around 10 months old.

Q When will my babies be able to manage finger foods?
A • Once your babies start to grab at the spoon, give them one each to hold.

• When they repeatedly put it in their mouths, load it up and let them try to get it into their mouths, quickly popping in any food that falls out with your own spoon.

- With a little help and guidance, most babies from 12 months are capable of feeding themselves part of their meal.
- Always supervise your babies during mealtimes: never, ever leave them alone.

Q When can I stop sterilising?

A • Bottles should be sterilised until your babies are one year old.

- Dishes and spoons can stop being sterilised when your babies are six months. They can then be put in the dishwasher, or washed thoroughly in hot soapy water, then rinsed and left to air-dry.

- Between four and six months the pots, cooking utensils and ice-cube trays used for preparing weaning food can either be put in the dishwasher or washed in hot soapy water, rinsed and then have boiled water poured over them before being left to air-dry.

Q Which foods are most likely to cause allergies, and what are the main symptoms?

A • The most common foods that cause allergies are dairy products, wheat, fish, eggs and citrus fruits.

- Symptoms include rashes, wheezing, coughing, running nose, sore bottom, diarrhoea, irritability and swelling of the eyes.

- Keeping a detailed record when you are weaning can be a big help in trying to pinpoint the cause of any of the above symptoms.

- These symptoms can also be caused by house mites, animal fur, wool and certain soaps and household cleaning agents.

- If in doubt, always check with your doctor to rule out any other possible causes or illness for these symptoms.

Useful addresses

Black-out lining and roller blinds
Available from all John Lewis Partnership stores throughout the UK.

Breast pumps
Ameda Egnell Ltd
Unit 2, Belvedere Trading Estate
Taunton
Somerset TA1 1BH
Tel: 01823 336 362

Baby equipment
The Great Little Trading Company
Pondwood Close
Moulton Park
Northampton NN3 6DF
Tel: 0870 850 6000
Fax: 01604 640 107

Blooming Marvellous
www.bloomingmarvellous.co.uk

Express Yourself Bras
www.expressyourselfbras.co.uk

SnoozeShade
Sun and sleep shades that help babies
nap-on-the-go. Give baby protection from
sun, wind, chill and light rain.
www.snoozeshade.com
01932 500427

Organisations

Twins and Multiple Births Association (TAMBA)
2 The Willows
Gardner Road
Guildford GU1 4PG
Tel (Twinline): 0800 138 0509
Tel (Office): 0870 770 3305
www.tamba.org.uk

Multiple Births Foundation
Hammersmith House, Level 4
Queen Charlotte's and Chelsea Hospital
Du Cane Road
London W12 0HS
Tel: 020 8383 3519
www.multiplebirths.org.uk
info@multiplebirths.org.uk

Foundation for the Study of Infant Deaths
Artillery House
11–19 Artillery Row
London SW1P 1RT
Tel: 020 7222 8001

Further reading

The Complete Sleep Guide for Contented Babies and Toddlers by Gina Ford (Vermilion, 2006)

The Contented Child's Food Bible by Gina Ford and Paul Sacher (Vermilion, 2004)

The Contented Little Baby Book of Weaning by Gina Ford (Vermilion, 2006)

The Contented Toddler Years by Gina Ford (Vermilion, 2006)

The Gina Ford Baby and Toddler Cook Book by Gina Ford (Vermilion, 2005)

The Great Ormond Street New Baby and Child Care Book (Vermilion, 2004)

Healthy Sleep Habits, Happy Child by Marc Weissbluth (Vermilion, 2005)

The New Baby and Toddler Sleep Programme by Professor John Pearce with Jane Biddler (Vermilion, 1999)

Potty Training in One Week by Gina Ford (Vermilion, 2006)

Remotely Controlled by Aric Sigman (Vermilion, 2005)

Sleep: The Secret of Problem-free Nights by Beatrice Hollyer and Lucy Smith (Cassell, 2002)

Solve Your Child's Sleep Problems by Richard Ferber (Dorling Kindersley, 1985)

What to Expect When You're Breast-feeding... And What If You Can't? by Clare Byam-Cook (Vermilion, 2006)

Index

Also by Gina Ford
Available from Vermilion

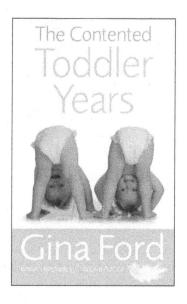

In *The New Contented Little Baby Book*, Gina Ford guides parents through their baby's first year. But as a baby grows, so his or her routines and patterns change. In *The Contented Toddler Years* Gina addresses the demands and needs of your growing toddler. From walking and talking, to teething and potty training, Gina offers her invaluable down-to-earth advice and insight into these crucial stages of your child's development.

The Contented
Little Baby
Book of
Weaning

Your one-stop guide
to contented
feeding

Gina Ford

Britain's Bestselling Childcare Author

Weaning your baby on to solid foods is one of the most important milestones during the early months of parenthood, and Gina's expert advice on weaning makes a baby's transition from milk to solid foods as straightforward as possible. Successful weaning establishes a pattern of healthy eating in babies, avoiding the pitfalls of fussy eaters restricted to a narrow diet.

In this revised edition of *The Contented Little Baby Book of Weaning*, Gina includes the latest recommendations regarding breast-feeding and the introduction of solid food from the World Health Authority and the UK Department of Health. She aims to take the worry out of weaning, guiding parents step-by-step through the process.

The
Complete
Sleep Guide
for Contented Babies
and Toddlers

Gina Ford

Britain's Bestselling Childcare Author

Sleep is one of the most misunderstood and confusing aspects of parenthood. While many babies fall naturally into a good sleeping pattern, latest research shows that the majority do not, leading to months, and sometimes years, of stressful, sleepless nights for children and parents. If your child has trouble sleeping or you simply wish to avoid sleep problems for your new baby now, and as it grows older, Gina Ford's practical step-by-step guide is the one for you. Gina's tried and tested methods will help you understand your children's sleep patterns and she gives you invaluable advice on how to avoid or resolve common problems.

Gina Ford knows from experience that one area of parenting that can be a big, scary hurdle for parents is potty training. The good news is that it's very easy when you know all the tips and tricks and there is no need for tantrums or endless hours spent sitting with a toddler who refuses to go potty.

With handy tips and anecdotes from parents who have been there, including advice on accidents, rewards and bed-wetting, *Potty Training in One Week* will help you do just that – and you won't have to tear your hair out in the process.

Britain's leading childcare author offers you her top tips for guaranteeing happy, healthy little babies . . .

Gina Ford guides you through the key stages of baby and toddler care including sleeping, weaning, feeding, potty training and behavioural development with her invaluable, sound and practical advice on parenting. This handy guide will fit in your handbag to make it quick and easy to access, wherever you are.

The
Contented
Baby with
Toddler Book
Gina Ford
Britain's Bestselling Childcare Author

One of the most exciting moments in a parent's life is introducing a toddler to their new baby brother or sister. But alongside the joy of having two young children comes the challenge of balancing their different needs.

The Contented Baby with Toddler Book is full of practical tips and brilliant solutions that will calm and support all busy parents. A major feature of the book is the easy-to-follow and adaptable routines, specifically designed to help you structure your day and meet all the needs of your toddler and your new baby . . . and still have time for lots of cuddles.

By using Gina's easy-to-follow methods not only will you have a contented baby who feeds regularly and sleeps through the night from an early age, but also a happy, involved toddler who remains calm and co-operative during this unsettled time.

Picking up where *The Contented Little Baby Book of Weaning* leaves off, *The Gina Ford Baby and Toddler Cook Book* addresses the next stage in childhood nutrition. Packed with nutritional advice and delicious recipes, its unique family-centred approach shows how it's possible for babies and their parents to enjoy the same meals together.

With over 100 recipes from classics like Shepherd's Pie to more unusual ideas such as Fruity Lamb Tagine and Gina's very own Bubble and Squeak Potato Cakes, all the recipes in this book are quick and easy to prepare. In her inimitable style, Gina also suggests clever time-saving devices to help fit good wholesome cooking into a busy family life; from adapting a single recipe to suit every family member through to batch cooking, and from creative use of leftovers through to quick finger foods.

The Gina Ford Baby and Toddler Cook Book is the perfect one-stop-guide for parents who want to feed their children delicious and healthy food and make family mealtimes a treat for everyone.

'With glossy pictures of happy, well-fed children and tasty recipes, this is an impressive package . . . It's all very yummy stuff' Junior